A Pictorial Guide to
THE MOUNTAINS OF SNOWDONIA

4. The Southern Peaks

A Pictorial Guide to
THE MOUNTAINS OF SNOWDONIA

4. The Southern Peaks

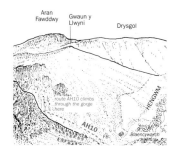

JOHN GILLHAM

F
FRANCES LINCOLN LIMITED
PUBLISHERS

*To my nephew and fellow author Roy Clayton,
who brought me back to the mountains*

The author intends to keep this book as up-to-date as possible,
and will offer information updates on his website:
www.johngillham.com

Frances Lincoln Limited
4 Torriano Mews
Torriano Avenue
London NW5 2RZ

*A Pictorial Guide to the Mountains of Snowdonia
Volume 4. The Southern Peaks*
Copyright © 2011 Frances Lincoln Limited

Text, photographs and 3D sketch maps
copyright © 2011 John Gillham
Edited by Roly Smith
Designed by Jane Havell Associates
First Frances Lincoln edition 2011

John Gillham has asserted his moral right to be
identified as Author of this Work in accordance
with the Copyright, Designs and Patents Act 1988

Contains Ordnance Survey data
© Crown copyright and database right 2010

British Library cataloguing-in-publication data
A catalogue record for this book is available from
the British Library
ISBN 978-0-7112-3136-8
Printed and bound in China
9 8 7 6 5 4 3 2 1

*Frontispiece: Descending the old quarry track into
Cwm Cywarch.*
Title page map: Blaen Cywarch

Contents

CONTENTS

CONTENTS

CONTENTS

CONTENTS

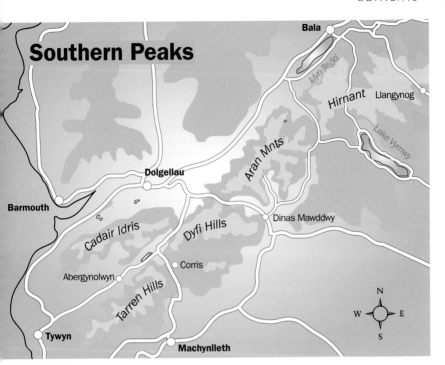

Southern Peaks

Bala

Llyn Tegid

Hirnant

Llangynog

Lake Vyrnwy

Aran Mnts

Dolgellau

Barmouth

Cadair Idris

Dyfi Hills

Dinas Mawddwy

Corris

Abergynolwyn

Tarren Hills

N

W   E

S

Tywyn

Machynlleth

The skies above Barmouth and Mawddach Estuary glowed, a cross between gold and silver, as the now calm surf glimmered in reflective mood. Our friends Phil and Sheila Iddon had joined Nicola and me on a weekend that would take in Cadair Idris and the Aran mountains, and we had intended to be somewhere in the middle by nightfall. But then the storm came.

Black skies – and horrendous rain coming from the clouds with the vengeance of an old Welsh warlord telling us to keep off the mountain. Perhaps it was King Arthur himself, for it is said that this was his seat. But here we were in our little tents getting hungrier by the minute as the aromas of Phil's rather wonderful stew-pot mingled with the bracing sea air.

Two beagles came bounding over the ridge, presumably following a scent trail laid down by their huntsmen masters. Heads to the ground, they had no time for us, or for the sunset. Half an hour later in the fading light the dogs were back, one still bounding and bright, the other, limping and less exuberant, as it trailed by a couple of minutes. As the dogs disappeared down towards the lakes of Cregennen, Barmouth came up with something we had no right to expect. Suddenly cascades of sparkling fireworks filled the night sky to the cracking and whistling of gunpowder. The people of the town were sharing their summer festival with us. Such evenings stay with you.

Cadair is one of Snowdonia's great places: the equal to Snowdon. It's softer and more gentle, with the greenery of surrounding meadows and woods, yet it still has the majesty that volcanoes and glaciers bring to the high places. Cadair has the sea, the sand and the sublime Mawddach Estuary. I've talked myself into it – Cadair is actually even finer than Snowdon.

We all made it on to the Aran ridge the next day. The Aran mountains are not as spectacular as those of Cadair Idris but they're still rugged with splendid cliffs and tarns on the eastern side. Cwm Cywarch, just a short way north of Dinas Mawddwy,

Opposite: Last light over the Mawddach Estuary and its long bridge taken during a memorable backpacking trip. Within minutes of this shot, a fireworks show started from Barmouth.

is perhaps their jewel. Again, the surroundings are softened with greenery but the contrast between the trees and farm pastures and the powerful climbers' buttresses of Craig Cywarch is awe-inspiring.

The Ordovician world of hard rock is tempered by the intervening ridges of the Dyfi and Tarren hills, for here they are rounded in profile, with grassy tops and shaley, broken crags. Both ranges have been spoiled in places by the vast, largely coniferous spread of the Dyfi Forest, which has crept up through the valleys high on to some of the hillsides; but both have little corners, their high points, where long easy ridges give wide views and even wider skies. With the Tarren it's usually Cadair and the Dyfi Estuary figuring in the views, while on the Dyfi hills it's the craggy Arans, the picturesque pastoral valleys and the soft, velvety hills east of the Dyfi.

Volume One of the series covers Northern Snowdonia. Here the 3000ft/900m Carneddau whaleback ridges vie for attention with those of the Glyderau, Wales's most rocky peaks, and Moel Siabod and the Nantgwynant Mountains, perhaps the least walked but the prettiest peaks in Snowdonia.

Volume Two includes Snowdon, the highest and most famous mountain in Wales, along with two not-so-well-known ranges, the Rhinogydd and Eifionydd. The former have been hewn from Cambrian grits older than any of the other Welsh mountains, while the latter have been fashioned by volcanoes and lava flows. Both offer enchanting seldom-trod routes for the connoisseur of fine scenery.

Volume Three covers Eastern Snowdonia, where the Migneint is more of a wilderness than any other area of the National Park; it's for lovers of solitude who don't mind wet feet. Only slightly less remote are the larger and rockier Arenig Mountains. The Moelwynion and Ffestiniog peaks have been ravaged but not tamed by the quarrymen and the miners. The sense of history is heightened as you pass long-abandoned barracks and the remains of old tramway bogies and pulleys. Finally, there are the long ridges and glacial rocky cwms of the Berwyns. Most of the peaks of the range are outside the National Park but they're too near, too big and too beautiful to be ignored.

Opposite: Maesglase, the highest of the velvety soft Dyfi hills, seen here from the head of Cwm Cerist.

I've divided the book up into three sections, one for each mountain group. For each mountain I've given various routes to the top, followed by ridge routes to the next peak. The combination of ascents and ridge routes allows readers to devise their own itineraries rather than blindly following the author's recommendations. The routes are numbered within each section, and the corresponding numbers are marked in yellow circles on the location maps at the beginning of each section. At the end of the section for each mountain range I've added a couple of big circular day-walks. These will take in the best of the mountains and also add some low-level link routes. If there are any extra navigational difficulties in descent I have made notes on these descents. **I must stress here that the times and distances given for each route are for ascents (one way) only.**

The panoramic drawings are not to scale and are no substitute for the recommended use of OS Explorer maps. In the interests of clarity, I've often raised or lowered a ridge and pulled 'out of sight' detail to the right or left a tad. Artistic licence is my advantage over modern digital imaging: I can see around a bend.

All the routes are safe for experienced walkers in clement conditions, but in wintry conditions even some of the most innocuous routes become dangerous and may be impassable. If these conditions are possible, take an ice axe and crampons, but first make sure you know how to use them. Be ready to turn around where necessary.

Remember, too, even the mountains change. A storm could have brought down a path across loose mountain scree or friable terrain; a bridge could have been washed away by those storms, or operations of some sort or another could have necessitated a diversion or closure of a path. River crossings can become difficult or even impossible after periods of snow or heavy rainfall and conifer plantations are forever changing. Spruce trees reach maturity and whole blocks are felled leaving behind hard-to-follow or diverted footpaths. Always be prepared to adjust your itinerary.

Opposite: The Aran ridge seen across Bala and its lake.

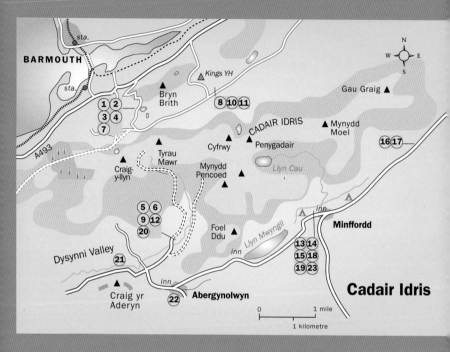

BARMOUTH

sta.

sta.

A493

Bryn Brith ▲

Kings YH ▲

Gau Graig ▲

① ②
③ ④
⑦

⑧ ⑩ ⑪

CADAIR IDRIS

Mynydd Moel ▲

Cyfrwy

Penygadair ▲

⑯ ⑰

Tyrau Mawr ▲

Mynydd Pencoed ▲

Llyn Cau

Craig-y-llyn ▲

⑤ ⑥
⑨ ⑫
⑳

Foel Ddu ▲

Llyn Mwyngil

inn

Minffordd

Dysynni Valley

㉑

inn

⑬ ⑭
⑮ ⑱
⑲ ㉓

Craig yr Aderyn ▲

inn

㉒ Abergynolwyn

Cadair Idris

0   1 mile

1 kilometre

'Old Cader is a grand fellow and shows himself superbly with ever-changing light. Do come and see him.' Thus wrote Charles Darwin to his colleague Sir Joseph Hooker in 1869. Rising out of the Mawddach Estuary like a great wall, the splintered northern cliffs of Cadair Idris are a magnificent sight, especially when dappled with the gold-pink light of a Welsh sunset. This most romantic of Welsh mountain ranges has been bathed in legend and myth since the early days of the Celtic bards.

THE PEAKS

Main Tops	height	
Penygadair	2929ft	893m
Mynydd Moel	2831ft	863m
Cyfrwy	2660ft	811m
Mynydd Pencoed	2594ft	791m
Gau Graig	2240ft	683m
Tyrau Mawr	2168ft	661m
Craig-y-llyn	2040ft	622m
Braich Ddu	1790ft	546m
Foel Ddu	1469ft	448m
Bryn Brith	1223ft	373m
Craig yr Aderyn	846ft	258m

It's no wonder this idyllic corner of Meirionnydd has attracted praise from poets and artists alike. Wordsworth described the view of Cadair Idris from the Mawddach Estuary as 'sublime and equal to that of any Scottish glen', while Richard Wilson's fine painting of 1765 hangs in Tate Britain in London.

Though not quite reaching the heights of central Snowdonia, Cadair is surely Wales's best hard rock mountain range, with all the grandeur of Snowdon and a little bit more. Towering over the soft sands and surf of the Mawddach Estuary and Cardigan Bay, it possesses fine crag-bound tarns, sheer rock faces and wide sweeping views across what seems like the whole of Wales. Unlike Snowdon, it's set in a green, fertile landscape, one with oak woods, dashing streams and pretty stone cottages dotted across pastoral foothills.

The range spans some 12 miles/19km alongside the southern shores of the Mawddach Estuary: rising in the west from the mile-long Barmouth Bridge and declining in the east to the backyards and slate rooftops of Dolgellau. The great northern cliffs you see are made up of granophyre, a particularly hard crystalline rock, which has resisted erosion while the softer rocks overlying them have been washed away.

Cadair Idris means the seat of Idris (Welsh for Arthur), but many writers over the years have taken the word seat too literally and have proclaimed the saddle between Cyfrwy and Penygadair to be the chair of Idris the giant. Idris was more likely to have been an offspring of Meirion, who founded Meirionnydd. Meirion's father was Cunedda, a Celtic warrior from Scotland, who in the fifth century drove the Irish out of these parts. Thus the area as a whole would have been their seat.

In describing Cadair country I'll start from the west and from the bottom of the hill, at little Arthog, a slate village not far from Barmouth Bridge. Arthog's all but in the woods, not the horrid spruce woods of the twentieth and twenty-first centuries, but ancient oak woods with leafy paths climbing to the plateau beneath those northern faces. Here you'll find the twin lakes of Cregennen, and one of the region's great little rock peaks, Bryn Brith.

Below: The Cadair Idris range seen from Barmouth across the Mawddach Estuary.

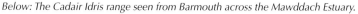

In the west the peaks are gentler, still steep-sided and with a little rock, but with easy, grassy ridges connecting bilberry-clad tops. The most westerly of the main peaks, Braich Ddu, lies above Arthog and Fairbourne. While it's grown a hairdo of spruce trees, Braich Ddu still displays a rock-strewn north face. This gives way to the crag-fringed two-thousand footer, Craig-y-llyn which, as the name suggests, cradles a small lake, Llyn Cyri. Viewed from Barmouth, the next peak, Tyrau Mawr, is the dominant one. Many, seeing its overhanging crags and distinctive shape, think it's the main peak, Penygadair, but this is further east, in the shadow of Cyfrwy.

Scurry down the other side of Tyrau Mawr to the pass of Rhiw Gwredydd and you'll almost certainly be met by a procession of walkers. They've climbed the popular slabbed Pony Path from Ty-nant. Ancient travellers would have crossed the pass and continued down towards Llanfihangel and Tywyn. Today's walkers, however, will be turning their backs to the west and continuing around the shoulder of Cyfrwy to Penygadair on their route to the top.

Walkers generally ignore Cyfrwy. There's no big path along the south-west spur, just a grind across boulders and scree. If those walkers would just make a detour eastwards from the Pony Path to Llyn y Gadair, they would see the Cyfrwy Arête. Soaring up from the back of the lake, it's a climbers' paradise.

The legendary nineteenth-century Dolgellau climber O. G. Jones learned his craft on Cadair Idris, and his first real climb was on this arête. Hard though it may be to believe, he scaled those near-vertical rock-faces solo, dressed in a suit and even without the nailed boots considered necessary at that time.

Penygadair, which rises to 2930ft/893m above sea level, is part of a more complex massif, with connecting ridges to Mynydd Pencoed, which overlooks Tal-y-llyn and the Dysynni Valley, and to Mynydd Pencoed above Tal-y-llyn. There's a trig point topping the summit rocks, and the remains of a stone hut just to the north-east. At Penygadair the ridge is at its narrowest and its slopes plunge on both sides to the grand ice-sculpted corrie lakes of Llyn y Gadair and Llyn Cau. Crags wrap themselves around Llyn Cau with only a narrow opening below the tarn's outflow.

You cannot but be impressed by Mynydd Pencoed, whose eastern side forms a conical rock-face rearing up from the head of the cwm. The rocks are dark and etched with the black shadows of two deep scree-strewn gullies. Continuing along the main ridge you come to Mynydd Moel, whose splintered cliffs match its larger neighbour, and a little lake, Llyn Arran, set amongst barren, stony ground to the north. The bold mountain sends out a broad bouldery southern spur, which all but encloses Cwm Cau and its lake.

Cadair's ridge finally gives out at Gau Graig, but like everything else it does, Cadair gives out in style, as anyone who has viewed the crag from the road above the Cross Foxes Inn will testify. Gau Graig's knobbly north-east spur has quite the most delightful path of the whole range. In late summer the crags are enhanced with the vivid purple of blooming heather.

The south side of Cadair is soft and green, like an Irish hillside. Usually you approach from Dolgellau, over the pass Bwlch Llyn Bach. Here the bold tarred road threads between the dusky towers of Craig y Llam and Mynydd Gwerngraig to reach the most beautiful lake in Wales, Llyn Mwyngil. (The OS calls this Tal-y-llyn Lake on current maps but, literally translated, this would mean 'end of the lake lake'!)

Llyn Mwyngil feeds the Afon Dysynni, which flows south-westwards through the slate-mining and forestry village of Abergynolwyn. Here the river seems to behave strangely for, although a fine green valley formed by the Bala Fault continues its way towards Tywyn, the river arcs right to squeeze into a narrow gorge between Foel Cae'rberllan and Gamallt. This phenomenon was caused in the last Ice Age, when the original line of river was blocked by ice, behind which a glacial lake formed until the river broke out along this new line.

We'll follow the new line now, for this will lead us to the Pennant Valley, Cadair's soft green underbelly, where the hills really are as rounded as the plumpest mummy's tummy. Well, all except one hill, that is. Craig yr Aderyn (Bird Rock) is small, but its shape is bold, bell-like on one side, with huge crags and screes tumbling down to the flat fields of the valley floor. Like most precipices, Craig yr Aderyn has a weakness, and you'll be able to ambush it from behind on fairly easy grass paths. The little summit is a great place for lounging and taking in the genteel beauty of field and farm.

Above: Storm over Cadair Idris. Cadair is a wonderful mixture of verdant pasture, woodland and craggy mountainside.

Seen from the north, Bryn Brith is just another of those rocky foothills running east to west beneath the main Cadair range – just a little ridge with two summits. From the shores of the Cregennen lakes, though, the foothill becomes a mountain, miniature maybe, but its bold ramparts rear up like an offspring of the Eiger and will issue an irresistible challenge to all able-bodied walkers.

Bryn Brith means the speckled hill, a strange name, maybe something to do with the rashes of stones and boulders on its slopes, or its dappling of heather. The OS Explorer map pastes another name, Pared y Cefn-hir, the wall on the long ridge, over the mountain's contours – just to confuse matters. I believe this to be the name of the ridge as a whole, with the wall referring to the tumbledown foundations of the ancient hill fort capping the west summit. The views from the fort are tremendous. To the north you look across the Mawddach Estuary and its mile-long railway bridge, and to the south across Cregennen, where Cyfrwy, Penygadair and Mynydd Moel all stand in perfect formation above the fields and the woods of Ty-nant.

Ridge is too precise a word for Pared y Cefn-hir, for soon you'll notice a small marshy hollow between the fort and a slightly higher, but less interesting, peak to the north. In the hollow there's a small, unnamed tarn, matching a larger tarn, Llyn Pen Moelyn, just beyond the more distant peak. The south ridge is hard work in places, with some quite steep drops into shady depressions.

Route C1
Llynnau Cregennen

A splendid little 'after tea' or 'before
*   Penygadair' route to get the juices flowing*
Start: Llynnau Cregennen car park
    (GR: SH 657143)
Distance: ½ mile/0.8km
Height gain: 425ft/130m
Time: ½ hour

The setting for the start of the walk is stunning with a full half-circle of craggy mountains, including the great wall of Cadair Idris and its satellites, forming an amphitheatre around the shimmering lakes of Cregennen. Bryn Brith is the nearest peak, the lowest perhaps but with soaring crags, which look impregnable from this angle.

Turn left out of the car park to follow the lane alongside the shores of the northern Cregennen lake. After a short way, turn right on a well-used path across rushy moorland to the north of the lake, before leaving this for a narrow path tackling Bryn Brith head on. The

Opposite: The bold ramparts of Bryn Brith soar above Llynnau Cregennen.

Above: View of Craig-y-llyn from Bryn Brith.

steep winding path scrambles over rock and heather – you'll need to use your hands in a couple of places – before reaching a fine airy summit and the walls of the old fort. It's one of the most exhilarating short scrambles in Snowdonia and you're rewarded with stunning views towards Cadair.

Route C2
Descent to Llynnau Cregennen
An easier route of descent to complete the circle

Start: Bryn Brith hillfort (GR: SH 663150)
Distance: 1¼ miles/2km
Height difference: 180m (descent), 40m ascent along ridge
Time: ½ hour

As it's likely you'll be tackling this hill as a short one-off route, I'll include a continuing itinerary along the ridge and an easier, less 'sporty' descent route to get you back to Cregennen.

From the fort, continue north-eastwards along the undulating rocky ridge, known as Pared y Cefn-hir. There's a shallow cwm with a tiny tarn to the left and a slightly higher but out-of-the-way peak (the ridge's highest point) on its far side.

By staying this side of the cwm the route descends into a grassy hollow. The seriousness of the south slopes has lessened by now and it is possible to descend right (south-east) on a narrow path. This eventually fades into rough pasture just above the main wallside right of way marked on the map (GR 670151). This takes you west back to the starting point by Cregennen's shores.

Other route options
It is possible to access the fell from the lane (GR 680157) just south-west of Kings Youth Hostel. A track, then a path, heads west to the fields of Ty'n-llidiart (note: the marked small conifer plantation doesn't exist) and climbs by the outflow stream of Llyn Pen Moelyn on to the ridge.

Below: Bryn Brith from Llynnau Cregennen.

CRAIG-Y-LLYN

Craig-y-llyn, the lake crag, and its subsidiary top, Braich Ddu, the black arm, are the most westerly of the major Cadair Idris summits. Rising from the sandbars and tides of the Mawddach Estuary and the mile-long railway bridge, these peaks are distinguished by their precipitous craggy northern faces.

Braich Ddu, the lesser peak, has in recent years been encroached upon by spruce plantations, although once you're clear of them, the easy ridge-walking offers a fine prelude to the more spectacular tops to the east. The ridge arcs almost 90 degrees as it encircles the deep grassy cwm separating Braich Ddu and Craig-y-llyn. Llyn Cyri, a small shallow tarn, basks here reflecting the pinks, greens and greys of Craig-y-llyn's sweeping slopes, which are vertically striated with vegetated crag and scree.

As is the case with many of Cadair's peaks, the mountain has gentle southern sides, with heather in the higher regions and moor grass lower down. These slopes are riven deep by the pastured cwm of Nant Caw, which leads to the Pennant Valley.

Craig-y-llyn's summit is grassy and unspectacular, but the views over Llyn Cyri and over the twin lakes of Cregennen to the Mawd-

Left: Craig-y-llyn and Llyn Cyri seen from Braich Ddu.

dach Estuary are exquisite. The subsidiary west summit is topped by a large Bronze Age cairn, Twll yr Ogof, which means hole cave – curiously, for there are no signs of a hole or a cave.

Opposite: View from Ffordd Ddu of Barmouth and the Mawddach Estuary.

Route C3
Braich Ddu and Llynnau Cregennen

A splendid route starting quite high, with panoramas all the way to the top

Start: Llynnau Cregennen car park (toilets) (GR: SH 657143)

Distance: 5 miles/8km

Height gain: 1640ft/500m

Time: 3 hours

If you've read the glossy brochures produced by the Wales Tourist Board you'll probably recognise Cregennen with its twin lakes, proud pines and precipices. It's a wonderful place set high above the Mawddach Estuary but still dominated by the cliffs of Cadair Idris. What better place to start a walk?

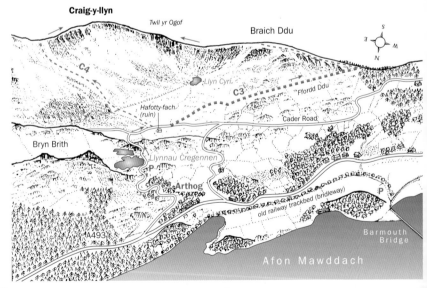

32

After turning right out of the car park, follow the lane past the shores of the northern lake before making a right turn at a T-junction. Beyond the ruins of Hafotty-fach, take the left fork, a stony track climbing the hillsides of Braich Ddu directly ahead. Views of the Mawddach Estuary, Barmouth and the declining southern Rhinog ridges reach panoramic proportions.

Another track joins in from the right, then you pass a memorial to the crew of a B-17 Flying Fortress which crashed here in 1945. Here a waymarker signpost directs you along another left fork, which cuts under the rocks of Braich Ddu before meeting a forestry plantation by a gate. Don't go through the gate here, but climb left along the perimeter fence to reach first Braich Ddu's summit then, after another steady climb, that of Craig-y-llyn.

Route C4
Direct route from Llynnau Cregennen
A stiff climb but the quickest way to the ridge
Start: Llynnau Cregennen car park
   (GR: SH 657143)
Distance: 2¼ miles/3.7km
Height gain: 1330ft/405m
Time: 1¼ hours

Turn right out of the car park and follow the lane past the shores of the bigger and more northerly lake, before turning right at the T-junction. Near the ruins of Hafotty-fach, leave the lane and cross a ladder stile in the wall on the left. Now follow a faint path across the first field to another stile at its far side. The route now climbs directly up the steepening slopes of the mountain, aiming for the col between Tyrau Mawr and Craig-y-llyn, with Tyrau Mawr's seemingly overhanging crags begging for attention on the left.

At the col go over the ladder stile before turning right to climb the grassy ridge up to Craig-y-llyn's summit.

Below: Craig-y-llyn from Tyrau Mawr ridge.

Route C5
Nant Caw and Trawsfynydd

A long trek with some stimulating views

Start: Llanfihangel-y-pennant car park
 (toilets) (GR: SH 672088)

Distance: 5 miles/8km

Height gain: 2100ft/640m

Time: 3 hours

The next two walks approach the mountain from its soft green southern side, through the pastures of Pennant and Nant Caw. While you're in the area you may wish to detour to back down the lane to see Prince Llewellyn's former stronghold, Castell y Bere, and Mary Jones's chapel, which stands just opposite the car park.

Parts of the chapel date back to the twelfth century. It is dedicated to Mary Jones, a poor weaver's daughter of the eighteenth century.

As a teenager she longed for her own bible. Though she had no shoes to wear, Mary trekked across the hills to Bala, which was some 30 miles/48km away. The Rev. Thomas Charles had no bibles to sell but, touched by her persistence, he gave her his own. Her act also inspired him to found the British and Foreign Bible Society.

Turn right out of the car park and follow the lane up the valley passing Mary's cottage, Tyn-y-ddol, before turning left just beyond the bridge over the Afon Cader. The farm track you're now following passes in front of the house at Gernos and continues westwards across fields close to the riverbank. Stay on this side of the river rather than crossing the concrete bridge by the farming complex of Maes-y-llan.

The river turns away and the path stays with a drystone wall on the right. Immedi-

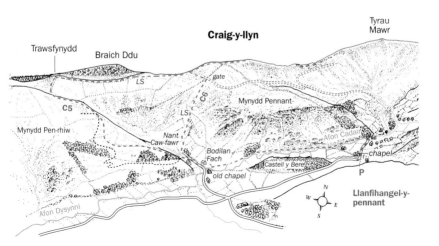

ately after passing an old chapel, turn left to ford a streamlet, beyond which you'll come to a narrow country lane. Turn right along the lane. After a short distance the lane terminates at Bodilan Fach farm. Continue along a surfaced farm lane towards a second farm, Nant-Caw-fawr, but leave this for the signposted bridleway on the left, a fine grass track zigzagging up the side of Mynydd Pen-rhiw. The view across the Dysynni Valley to Craig yr Aderyn (Bird Rock) can be stunning in good light.

Follow the waymarks and ignore the first left fork track to climb above two small conifer copses. The track climbs across pastures and turns sharp right, soon to be joined by a more prominent track from the left for a short way. You're now high above the deep hollow of Nant Caw. Take the right fork to stay close to the Nant Caw edge.

After being joined by a zigzag track from the bottom of the hollow (GR 645101), the track comes to a gate at the col between Esgair Berfa and Trawsfynydd. Beyond the gate it fades into the rushes and moor grasses. Here, turn right and climb by the fence on the right across the undistinguished thistle-entangled ridge of Trawsfynydd. Beyond a ladder stile the terrain improves again as you turn left alongside a fence at the edge of a field full of clover (and busy with bees in summer). Cross the ladder stile when you reach the ridge fence and turn right to climb the steady slopes past the ancient cairn on Twll yr Ogof to Craig-y-llyn's summit.

Below: The track above Nant Caw with the Dysynni Valley and the Tarren Hills in the background.

Above: On the track climbing out of Nant Caw. Castell y Bere is on the far right of the valley, its rocky knoll surrounded by trees.

Route C6
Nant Caw and Graig Lwyd

A long trek with stimulating views – complex route-finding

Start: Llanfihangel-y-pennant car park
  (GR: SH 672088)
Distance: 4¼ miles/7km
Height gain: 2035ft/620m
Time: 2¾ hours

As in Route C5 turn right out of the car park and follow the lane up the valley passing Mary Jones's chapel, then her cottage, Ty'n-y-ddol. Further up the lane just beyond the bridge over the Afon Cader, turn left on a farm track passing in front of the house at Gernos, before continuing across fields close to the riverbank. Stay on this side of the river rather than crossing the concrete bridge by the farming complex of Maes-y-llan.

Where the river turns away, the path stays with a drystone wall on the right. Immediately after passing an old chapel turn left and ford a streamlet to come out at a narrow country lane. Turn right past the farm at Bodilan Fach and continue up the surfaced farm lane to Nant Caw-fawr farm. Now you've entered the verdant if austere cwm of Nant Caw and the slopes of Mynydd Pen-rhiw and Mynydd Pennant are beginning to shut out the wide landscapes you've been seeing so far.

Above: High above Nant Caw with Esgair Berfa behind.

Take the mud-and-stone track to the left of the buildings and continue for a short way before going over a ladder stile (the first of many) on the right. Climb diagonally (northwards) across the first two fields, then maintain direction, past a ruin (the next ladder stile will always be in view). The route meets a grassy track and follows it for a short way. Where the track bends right, leave it and climb through bracken to another ladder stile by some substantial stone-built sheep pens.

A waymarker arrow highlights the direction up rough pathless slopes. Keep just above the ravines cut by streams, then head for the gate on the horizon. The gate lies at the end of a bulldozed track (GR 657112). Beyond it the track becomes a grass track heading across high pastures towards the col between Craig-y-llyn and Braich Ddu. Where it fades into the grass and clover, maintain your direction to the ridge then turn right alongside the fence to reach the summit.

Descent

The ridge is simple but waymarking on this route does not exist in reverse. On reaching the col between Braich Ddu and Craig-y-llyn head south-east, aiming for the gate at the head of a bulldozed track. Through this, look for the substantial sheepfolds near a large patch of bracken (they look like a ruined cottage from here). Aim for them, keeping the ravines of the streams below you and on the right.

Over the ladder stile beyond them cross some more bracken patches, follow a wide grass track for a short way, leaving it for a stile down on the right. Now you head SSW, linking ladder stiles to cross several fields.

Soon the farmhouse of Nant Caw-fawr, your next target, appears below you. Cut diagonally across the steep gradients of the bottom field to locate the riverside ladder stile, which lies by a track leading to the farm. Here follow the farm lane, then the public road past Bodilan Fach, and turn left by an old chapel. After fording a streamlet continue on a rough-in-places field path by a drystone wall. Follow a course parallel to the Afon Cadair, passing in front of the house at Gernos to reach the road. Turn right along this, passing Mary Jones's cottage at Ty'n-y-ddol back to the car park.

Other route options

If you are doing the western ridges you could start from Barmouth, crossing the Mawddach Estuary by the Barmouth Bridge. There's a series of quarry tracks and paths from south of the Arthog Bog Nature Reserve (GR 630135) climbing among wooded slopes, past the farm of Cyfannedd-fawr to the end of the Cadair Idris mountain road (GR 631120). Take the forestry track heading eastwards, eventually across open fell, then double back on the old Ffordd Ddu track to follow Route C3 up the Braich Ddu ridge and onwards to Craig-y-llyn.

RIDGE ROUTE

Tyrau Mawr

Distance: 1¼ miles/2 km
Height gain: 560ft/170m
Time: ¾ hour

The ridge fence guides you all the way along grassy ridges. There's quite a steep climb to Tyrau Mawr but you are rewarded with splendid views down rocky gullies. Once on the summit, you will be tempted to continue over the whole range, which is spread before you.

Tyrau Mawr (incorrectly shown as Tyrrau Mawr on OS maps) means the great towers, and viewing its northern face from the old Cader Road you can see why. From relatively soft green laneside slopes, the mountain grows bold, with overhanging cliffs and spiky tors glowering down over flowing screes.

Postcard views taken from the shores of the Cregennen lakes proclaim this to be Cadair Idris itself – even the OS map calls it Craig-las, a name referring only to the cliffs. The map shows Tyrau Mawr as an afterthought, placing it on the gentle grass slopes of the southern flanks. Perhaps they give 'Tyrau' the extra 'r' to make up for the indignity?

Of all Cadair Idris's western summits, Tyrau Mawr is the best. There's the excitement of the edge, as you look down from the ridge over spectacular gullies and tors. Its exposed summit gives fascinating and intricate views over fields, woods and little craggy hills, then across the Mawddach Estuary and the sweep of Cardigan Bay to what seems like the whole of Snowdonia. When this all gets too much, you can lie down on luxuriant beds of grass and reach out to the equally luxuriant beds of bilberry for sweet refreshment.

Most walkers tackle Tyrau Mawr as part of a ridge walk. One of the classics is the complete northern ridge of Cadair starting on the Barmouth Bridge and finishing at the Cross Foxes Inn. My favourite, however, is to do the mountain on its own from the north. Walk it on a late summer afternoon and early evening, watch the setting sun cast a silver, then golden, glow over the Mawddach, and you will have experienced the very best of this fine mountain.

Opposite: Looking down Tyrau Mawr's craggy towers to the Mawddach Estuary and the Rhinogydd. Right: Camping on Tyrau Mawr.

Route C7
Llynnau Cregennen and the northern slopes
The toughest, but the quickest and most
rewarding route
Start: Llynnau Cregennen car park
(GR: SH 657143)
Distance: 2¾ miles/4.5km
Height gain: 1425ft/435m
Time: 1½ hours

Cregennen is the best place to begin the ascent of this great peak, for Tyrau Mawr's great northern face, its flowing screes and rock-towered fringe are truly memorable from this vantage point.

From the car park follow the lane past Cregennen's shores towards Tyrau Mawr. After turning right at the T-junction, head for the roadside ruins of Hafotty-fach. Here cross a ladder stile in the wall on the left and aim for another stile at the far side of the rough field. A narrow path struggles up the steepening grass slopes of the mountainside but your toil is compensated by superb views back to Cregennen, the Mawddach Estuary and the Rhinog mountains beyond.

The sketchy path soon reaches the col between Tyrau Mawr and Craig-y-llyn, where you can look across to the verdant pastured hillsides surrounding the Afon Cadair and Dysynni valleys. Once over a ladder stile in the ridge fence, climb left up steep slopes to Tyrau Mawr's summit. En route you'll pass some pretty spectacular places at the heads of deep gullies. Ladder stiles allow you to cross to the edge at opportune moments.

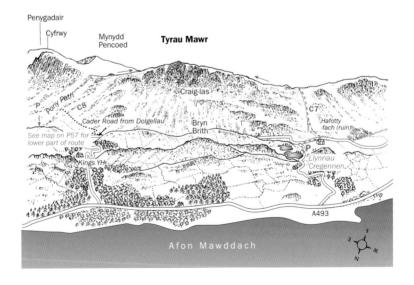

Route C8
The Pony Path from Ty-nant

The classic way up Tyrau Mawr if you haven't used the Pony Path to Penygadair before

Start: Ty-nant car park (GR: SH 698153)
Distance: 2½ miles/4 km
Height gain: 1675ft/510m
Time: 1½ hours

Splendid broadleaved woods, a swift and crystal stream and a fine one-arched stone bridge make Ty-nant an idyllic place, and all this greenery is wonderfully counterbalanced by the stark, columnar cliffs of Cyfrwy, which overlook the scene.

Out of the car park turn right along the lane, then left by a telephone box, where the Pony Path follows a shallow stream. The way-marked route passes to the right the pretty stone-built Ty-nant farm before climbing south-west by pleasant woodland, then beneath the impressive cliffs of Cyfrwy. At a gate in the intake wall, ignore the path on the left – it's going to Llyn y Gadair at the foot of those cliffs. Instead, maintain your direction on the more prominent path climbing towards the nick between Cyfrwy and Tyrau Mawr.

Some engineered zigzags make easy work of the steep slopes to Rhiw Gwredydd where you join the ridge. Now the bouldery slopes

Below: Tyrau Mawr's north face seen across Llynnau Cregennen.

43

of Cyfrwy rear up in whaleback fashion to your left, but you turn your back on this and climb the more grassy ridge to Tyrau Mawr – an entertaining climb with increasingly good views down precipices to the right. After passing the cairns and rocks of Carnedd Lwyd, the route reaches Tyrau Mawr's summit.

Right: On Tyrau Mawr with Penygadair and Cyfrwy ahead.

Route C9
Llanfihangel-y-pennant

*The long way up – saving the mountain's
  grandeur until the end*

Start: Llanfihangel-y-pennant car park
  (GR: SH 672088)

Distance: 5 miles/8km

Height gain: 2130ft /650m

Time: 2½ hours

Out of the car park turn right along the quiet lane, passing a couple of cottages, then going over the bridge across the Afon Cadair (Cader). The little road accompanies the babbling tree-lined stream to Gwastadfryn farm. Beyond the gate here it becomes a rough track, climbing gradually through the upper valley.

Tyrau Mawr lies ahead, but if it were a film star it would turn the other way, for its south face is featureless and uninteresting. It's all very pretty round here though, with Craig Ysgiog offering the excitement of some rock among the bracken and woodland, and the soaring slopes of Mynydd Pencoed dominating. The area has some history, too – many historians say Prince Llewellyn's brother Dafydd hid out hereabouts when he was forced to flee from the stronghold at Castell y Bere.

Leave the track at the second of two ladder stiles on the right (the first path, which is not signposted, just goes down to the river, where it ends). The second is a delightful grassy path, which descends gradually to an attractive slabbed packhorse bridge over a tributary

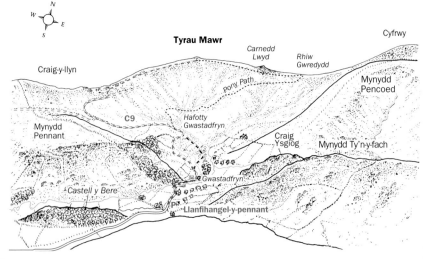

of the Afon Cadair. A stony path then climbs above the far banks before turning left by a wall. It rejoins the original track south of Hafotty Gwastadfryn.

At Hafotty Gwastadfryn, go through the gate on the left (the Pony Path uses the one on the right) and follow the track rounding the upper cwm. Ignore the next left fork, which traverses the south side of Craig-y-llyn. Leave your track as it levels off beneath the col west of Tyrau Mawr and climb the short pathless section to the ridge. Turn right here up the steep slopes to the summit.

RIDGE ROUTES

Penygadair
Distance: 2½ miles/4km
Height gain: 1125ft/340m
Time: 1½ hours

It's an easy-paced descent on a grassy ridge past the rocks and cairns of Carnedd Lwyd to the pass of Rhiw Gwredydd, where the Pony Path cuts across the ridge. A wide track climbs the breast of Cyfrwy towards Penygadair. It's on grass at first but the terrain becomes more bouldery as height is gained. Suddenly the path comes to an arête high above the rocky cwm of Llyn y Gadair, where you continue east along the cairned track to the trig point and summit cabin.

Cyfrwy
Distance: 2 miles/3.2km
Height gain: 855ft/260m
Time: 1¼ hours

Follow the previous ridge route to the pass of Rhiw Gwredydd, then follow the popular Pony Path alongside the ridge fence up the first part of Cyfrwy. Leave the main route where the fence turns away left and the ground ahead steepens. Head straight up the scree-strewn spur to the wind shelter and cairn on Cyfrwy's summit.

Craig-y-llyn
Distance: 1¼ miles/2km
Height gain: 425ft/130m
Time: ¾ hour

There's a steady descent along a fence-side grass path to the col before an equally steady climb to the higher north-eastern summit of Craig-y-llyn.

All Cadair's western ridges have so far been grassy. True, the rock begins to break out on Tyrau Mawr's northern face but, in general, these are amiable, free-striding hills. On Cyfrwy things get more serious. Along the rising ridge the grass is soon replaced by stone, then the stone by boulder. Splintered and columnar cliffs, divided by numerous gullies, plummet hundreds of feet to fans of scree and grassy moraine humps lying high above the Mawddach.

Cyfrwy rises from the back of Llyn y Gadair like a steely grey cone, with its arête a jagged stairway to the top. The mountain's name, which means the saddle, has encouraged some people to claim it to be the chair of Idris. Well, if it is the chair, there's also a table. The flat-topped obelisk is just over halfway down the narrow arête.

With all this grandeur you might well wonder why Cyfrwy's summit is not often visited by walkers. The answer is that it's not much more than half a mile from the higher Penygadair, and off-route too. Come here on a clear day and you will leave the crowds behind and enjoy the finest view of Penygadair's rugged north face, towering above the wild scree-strewn cwm of Llyn y Gadair.

Opposite: Cyfrwy as seen from the connecting ridge with Penygadair.

The mountain, like most in the Idris range, has its soft side, this one facing south-west. These slopes of stone and grass decline to the banks of the Afon Cadair some 2000ft/600m below. They're a mirror image of Mynydd Pencoed's northern slopes, which face Cyfrwy across an unnamed wild green hollow whose only real feature is a secretive waterfall shaded by some crags.

Cyfrwy is almost always tackled en route to Penygadair. Direct routes would involve a climb up its northern cliffs or a rather contrived slog up its western slopes from Hafotty Gwastadfryn. On reaching the pass of Rhiw Gwredydd it is possible to deviate from the Pony Path and stay closer to the northern edge but, due to the concave upper slopes, this would not afford a better view. There is one route, however, that gives to Cyfrwy the dignity of a direct ascent it deserves.

Below: The Cyfrwy arête seen from the Foxes Path, showing the Table halfway up.

Route C10
Llyn Gwernan and the Foxes Path
A dramatic approach route
Start: Gwernan Lake Hotel (GR: SH 704158).
    Car parking at Ty-nant (GR: SH 697153)
Distance: 4½ miles/6.8km (from the car park)
Height gain: 2490ft/760m
Time: 2½–3 hours

The short track eastwards from the car park at Ty-nant to the Gwernan Lake may be along the tarmac of the Cader Road but it's a quiet road, and very pretty too, with glimpses of Cyfrwy's rock walls through tree boughs and over laneside crags. In summer the lake surface is covered with water lilies.

The route proper begins at a gate opposite the whitewashed hotel. Beyond it a fine grass path climbs steadily through bracken, with rocky knolls rising to the left and the green fields of Tyddyn-mawr dropping to the right.

After a few minutes you'll see a small cottage on the right. The green dotted line on the map suggests you should turn right behind this, but in reality the Foxes Path climbs ahead (south-east). The two routes rejoin at a gate by some sheepfolds. The scenery becomes more rugged as height is gained and the crags are now interspersed with heather, hawthorn and a little gorse.

Llyn yr Gafr hides away until you're not 30 yards/m from its shores. Its waters are dark, shallow and spiked with rushes, and its immediate environs are overshadowed by the cliffs of Mynydd Moel. If it's a sunny August day, this romantic austerity will be tempered

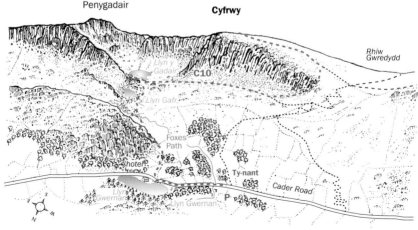

by the vivid purple pinks of the surrounding heather slopes.

A steep path now crosses the outflow stream and scrambles up stony ground to Llyn y Gadair, where splintered rocks and boulders surround the shoreline. Look left to Penygadair and you'll see the vast pinkish scree slopes of the Foxes Path. This once popular route to Cadair's summit is an unpleasant and hazardous undertaking these days because of erosion– so don't bother with it. We'll turn the other way for our route to Cyfrwy, whose magnificent cliffs may well be echoing to the banter of climbers, the clanking of their ironmongery and the sound of tumbling loose scree.

Follow Llyn y Gadair's western shore until you see a path heading away to the right. It will follow a low ridge of rock and grass running parallel to the base of Cyfrwy's screes. This rocky rampart was left here by the last Ice Age.

There's a confusing network of paths leading to the base of some of the climbs. The path you want is undulating and makes one steep descent to the right. The main thing to remember is to keep below the scree slopes and not bother too much if you lose the path when it hides beneath boulder heaps – you'll pick it up later and, if you look ahead to the grassy bits, you'll be able to make it out.

Cyfrwy's cliffs are always fascinating in these stages, though there are also delectable views down to the Mawddach. The going gets easier when the rocky ground is left behind and the path follows a grassy channel with low, grassy moraine hills to the right and the now lower cliffs to the left. Watch out for a division in the paths. The more prominent path (though still of sheep-track proportions) heads for the Pony Path, but the one we want here is the left fork, which keeps a little higher.

Where Cyfrwy's cliffs end you'll see another fork in the paths. Again you want the left fork, a tiny worn path through bilberry. It heads for a steep hillslope capped by a little crag and with a tiny and shallow scree gully. The little path goes left of the scree, crosses a broken wall and a parallel line of fenceposts before coming to a newer fence. Follow this uphill towards the Pony Path, but where it levels off turn half-left and climb up Cyfrwy's stony spur to the summit.

Other route options

Some of the finest routes up Cyfrwy are rock climbs and so unfortunately outside the scope of this book. The obvious other route is the Pony Path from Ty-nant diverting off left on reaching the pass at Rhiw Gwredydd for the direct path up Cyfrwy's rocky slopes.

RIDGE ROUTES

Penygadair

Distance: ½ mile/800m
Height gain: 385ft/120m
Time: 25 minutes

From the shelter on the stony summit it is a simple matter of following the rocky rim of Llyn y Gadair's cwm to meet the upper section of the Pony Path route. Follow this cairned path through boulders to the summit of Penygadair.

Tyrau Mawr

Distance: 2 miles/3.2km
Height gain: 330ft/100m
Time: 1¼ hours

Descend westwards down the stony slopes. The Pony Path, which has descended the southern breast of the mountain, will join your route from the left and take you down to the pass at Rhiw Gwredydd. A clear path then climbs grassy flanks, past the cairn and rocks of Carnedd Lwyd to Tyrau Mawr's summit.

Left: Llyn y Gafr as seen from the Foxes Path.

PENYGADAIR

The western ridges and summits of Cadair Idris I have described so far have been uncomplicated, with cliffs on the glaciated northern faces and grassy slopes to the south. The change starts on Cyfrwy, but at Cadair's highest summit, Penygadair, the transformation becomes complete. In Cwm Cau (the shut-in cwm) to the south a huge glacier has carved out a spectacular cragbound, lake-filled corrie. There's a matching one, that of Llyn y Gadair, lying around 1000 feet/300 metres below the north face too. This is glacial perfection.

Penygadair means hill of the chair, another reference to the legend of Idris the giant. The summit itself is a jumble of boulders topped by a trig point. Just a few paces away to the north there's a stone-built refuge shelter complete with a roof. Though it's often wet inside, it's a welcome sight on inclement days.

An original hut, built in the nineteenth century by Dolgellau man Richard Pugh, was an altogether more flimsy affair. From here an elderly lady served teas to visitors who were brought up the mountain by local guides. It is said that each morning she would be up with the lark and would rush up the mountain with her wares.

Left: Llyn Cau from the top of the Stone Shoot.

1. CADAIR IDRIS

In 1871 Pugh's son guided famous diarist Francis Kilvert up Cadair. They trudged up through incessant rain. Kilvert must have been depressed by the conditions, for he wrote that this was 'the stoniest, dreariest, most desolate mountain I was ever on'. Perhaps the guide felt some sympathy for his soaked companion because as they reached the summit he pointed out the Ordnance Survey's pile of stones: 'The Captain of the surveying company had his tent pitched on the top of Cader Idris for three summer months and never left the place. He had eighteen men to wait upon him. And how many clear views do you think he got in that time? Nine.'

By saving your walk for a clear day, and whatever Pugh said there are many each year, you will be rewarded by some of the finest views in Wales. I've mentioned the two cwms, each filled with an apple-shaped tarn. Though these take centre-stage there are many worthy sideshows.

Down below the wooded foothills to the north, the pale blue Mawddach lazily makes its way amid long golden sandbars to the sea. On the other side the sprawling hills of the southern Rhinogydd decline from the rockfaces of Diffwys to the little knobbly tors above Barmouth. Though it's more distant than the view from Tyrau Mawr or Craig-y-llyn, the extra height gives a new and impressive scale. Far horizons reveal the hazy hills of the Lleyn Peninsula and northern Snowdonia, while the bastion of Central Wales, Pumlumon, peeps through a gap in the afforested Tarren Hills.

Route C11
Ty-nant and the Pony Path
The easiest way which, though lacking the grandeur of some other routes, has some pretty riverside stretches
Start: Ty-nant car park (GR: SH 697153)
Distance: 3 miles/5km
Height gain: 2430ft/740m
Time: 2½ hours

The delightful picnic spot and car park at Ty-nant will be remembered for its splendid woods and lovely stream, which flows clear and fast over a stony bed. Out of the car park, turn right over the one-arched stone bridge, Pont Dyffrydan, and along the lane for a short way. Go left by a telephone box, where the Pony Path runs up alongside a shallow stream.

Go through a kissing gate next to the farmhouse at Ty-nant, cross the bridge over the stream and continue through woods including ash, birch and hazel. Above the woods a marker post highlights the way to the right across another stream bridge beneath the impressive cliffs of Cyfrwy. At a gate in the intake wall, maintain your direction on a prominent slabbed path climbing towards the nick between Cyfrwy and Tyrau Mawr. Some zigzags make easy work of the final steep slopes to Rhiw Gwredydd.

The path now turns left and climbs the breast of Cyfrwy. As you gain height the terrain becomes rockier. Hints of something spectacular in the offing come from the right where Mynydd Pencoed's pointed east

Above: Pont Dyffrydan at the start of the Pony Path.

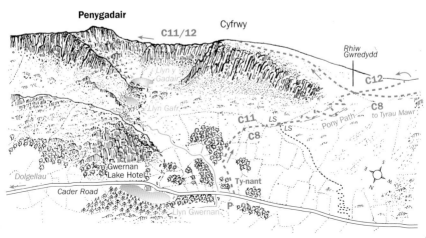

summit rises from the grass slopes of Daear Fawr to reveal the upper face of Craig Cau. The hint turns into a promise fulfilled as the now cairned path comes upon the edge of Llyn y Gadair's deep cwm, beyond which Penygadair's north face strikes up into the sky. An exciting path clambers between the rocks for a final summit push.

Descent

As long as you locate the start of the right fork path above the cwm of Llyn y Gadair there should be no problems – the left fork Minffordd Path will round Cwm Cau towards Mynydd Pencoed. At Rhiw Gwredydd, the pass between Cyfrwy and Tyrau Mawr, remember to take the zigzagging path on the right through the gate.

Route C12
The Pony Path from Llanfihangel-y-pennant

A long gentle route showing the verdant side of Cadair Idris

Start: Llanfihangel-y-pennant car park (GR: SH 672088)
Distance: 5 miles/8km
Height gain: 2860ft/870m
Time: 3 hours

Turn right out of the car park, past the church and along the quiet lane through the upper Pennant Valley. After crossing the bridge over the Afon Cadair you'll see the ruins of Mary Jones's cottage, Ty'n-y-ddol, and a monument to her in the shade of some trees. Beyond this the lane crosses Afon Cadair and follows its pretty tree-lined banks to Gwastadfryn farm,

Right: The valley of Afon Cadair showing Cadair Idris at its head.

where it ends. From here the route follows a rough track, climbing gradually across the lower slopes of Mynydd Pennant.

Watch out for the signed Pony Path, which goes over the second of two ladder stiles to the right of the track. A pleasant grass path descends gradually to a stream, which it crosses using a slabbed packhorse bridge. A stony path continues the climb up the far banks before turning left by a wall. The path rejoins the original track then follows it to Hafotty Gwastadfryn, once an old summer dwelling but now a large complex of sheep and cattle pens. Go over a ladder stile next to a gate and a blue waymarker, and follow the well-defined track across a stream.

The winding track now climbs the grassy southern flanks of Tyrau Mawr. Take the way-marked right fork at the next junction and head for the high pass of Rhiw Gwredydd. Here you meet an intersection of fences where you turn right over a stile and follow the Ty-nant path (Route C11) up the stony shoulder of Cyfrwy to the summit.

Descent

As in Route C11, locating the path forking right above the rim of Cwm y Gadair is the key. South of Hafotty Gwastadfryn, at GR 678114, watch out for the waymarker arrow on the left of the track.

Note: if you are in a hurry, it is quite permissible to follow the track all the way down to the lane at Llanfihangel.

Route C13
The Minffordd Path

The classic route up Cadair Idris
Start: Minffordd car park (GR: SH 732116)
Distance: 2¾ miles 4.4 km
Height gain: 2885ft/880m
Time: 2¾ hours

The wide path begins at a kissing gate beyond the toilet block and threads through an avenue of fine horse-chestnut trees before turning left and passing the National Trust information centre at Ystradgwyn. Beyond another gate you enter woodland, which has flourished here since the end of the last Ice Age some 10,000 years ago. It consists mainly of oak, but there are also limes, rowans and beech. Now managed as a National Nature Reserve, the woods have been fenced off to keep those 'woolly locusts', the sheep, out. The path, now a series of man-made wooden steps, climbs steeply through the trees, always with the boisterous white waters of Nant Cadair for company.

Beyond the woods you climb into Cwm Cau with the scree slopes of Mynydd Moel visible ahead. After swinging left into the heart of the cwm its great amphitheatre of rock surrounds you, but its lake, Llyn Cau, stays hidden behind grassy humps. These are moraines, left by the retreating glacier. The glacier was also responsible for depositing the many huge erratic boulders hereabouts.

Where the path divides, take the left fork, Route C14 (the right heads straight for the lake). More steps take you up towards the ridge. Among the moor grasses here you may

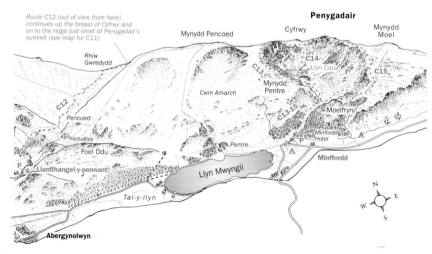

Above: The start of the Minffordd Path with Penygadair on the central horizon and Mynydd Pencoed to the left.

see the tiny yellow tormentil, but little else as the sheep graze freely here. In the fenced enclosures you'll see species such as bilberry and heather regenerating. Around the steeper ground of the rock outcrops of the cwm where the sheep don't go you may spot the delicate leafless stem and little white flowers of the starry saxifrage or maybe the blue-purple globe-flowered devil's bit scabious. Both love the alkaline soils leached from the volcanic rocks.

Llyn Cau soon comes into view, dwarfed by the buttresses and dark gullies of Craig Cau. It's not unlike Yr Wyddfa (Snowdon) and its upper lake, Glaslyn, but in this scene there's a little more greenery.

The ridge to Mynydd Pencoed's east summit above Craig Cau is a rocky one, but the path is always clear. There are glimpses down to Llyn Mwyngil. As you gain height the memorable scenes are in the other direction, where tremendous gullies plummet down to Llyn Cau.

Cross the ladder stile over the fence on the east summit of Mynydd Pencoed, then descend to the col lying between here and the highest peak, Penygadair. There's a choice of two paths, one closer to the edge of Cwm Cau than the other. Down to your left you should be able to see the green Pennant valley. The distinctive-shaped little hill in the mid-distance is Craig yr Aderyn (Bird Rock).

The path up to Penygadair soon leaves the edge of the cwm to climb over rock outcrops and boulders. Finally, it joins the Pony Path route just before the summit.

Descent

Be careful to locate the start of the path descending south-west away from the northern cliffs. It is easy to mistake the Minffordd Path for the cairned Pony Path, which follows the rim of Llyn y Gadair's cwm. Halfway up the ascent to Mynydd Pencoed's east summit, ignore the path forking right above the line of a fence. This is a shortcut to the Pencoed's west summit and Cwm Amarch.

Opposite: Cwm Cau and the rocky face of Mynydd Pencoed from the path on the east side.

Route C14
Cwm Cau and the Stone Shoot

A splendid alternative for the confident
Start: Minffordd car park (GR: SH 732116)
Distance: 2½ miles/4km
Height gain: 2605ft/795m
Time: 2½ hours

This exhilarating alternative for experienced walkers in good conditions begins in the same fashion as the Minffordd Path, which sets off through a kissing gate beyond the toilet block and passes along an avenue of fine horse-chestnut trees before turning left and past Ystradgwyn. Beyond another gate the route enters woodland, and climbs a series of wooden steps, with the rushing waters of Nant Cadair down to the right.

Beyond the woods the path enters Cwm Cau, with the scree slopes of Mynydd Moel visible ahead. After swinging left into the heart of the cwm its great amphitheatre of rock surrounds you, then Llyn Cau, a classic glacial tarn, comes into view.

The Minffordd Path is the main left fork, but on this route you should ignore it and go straight ahead towards the shores of Llyn Cau. Turn right and follow the lakeshore path beneath Penygadair's south face. A stony path meanders up steep slopes towards the col between Mynydd Pencoed and Penygadair. The final stages are very steep indeed but strong walkers will be rewarded by the intimate views of Pencoed Pillar and the fine gullies surrounding it.

Note: This is not recommended as a descent.

Route C15

East of Cwm Cau

A fine route completing the Cwm Cau circle

Start: Minffordd car park (GR: SH 732116)

Distance: 2¾ miles 4.4km

Height gain: 2655ft/810m

Time: 2½ hours

Again, this route starts along the Minffordd Path. From the toilet block at the back of Minffordd's car park follow the Cadair Idris signs. The well-defined path takes you through an avenue of trees, then left past Ystradgwyn before winding and climbing steeply through oak woods into open mountainside. Here you leave the path to ford Nant Cadair, beyond which a narrow path climbs north-west up the grassy north side of Moelfryn.

After going over a ladder stile straddling a wall, turn left and follow the wall on a loose stony path up steep slopes. Beyond a second ladder stile the path becomes steeper and horribly eroded with loose stones everywhere. The struggle ends beyond a third ladder stile. Although the eroded path continues by the fence and is the quickest way to the summit, sensible walkers will turn left here to cross the stile before climbing along a narrow path exploring the east side of Cwm Cau. The view you get in the middle stages reveals this glacial hollow to perfection. Equally impressive is the view of Tal-y-llyn with Llyn Mwyngil languishing in pastures beneath Graig Goch.

In the middle stages the going gets a little wetter as the path weaves among rocks and crosses some springs, but the difficulties are

short-lived as you traverse the firm southern slopes of Mynydd Moel to join the main ridge path. Now you just follow the firm ridge towards Penygadair. The path steepens and the terrain becomes bouldery as you approach the summit.

Descent

The path begins inconspicuously from the lower right of two ridge paths from Penygadair – a cairn marks the spot. You'll see the path swinging right to traverse the slopes of Mynydd Moel.

Above: The faint right fork track shown here is the key to the descent on Route C15.

Other route options

In times gone by, the Foxes Path from Llyn y Gadair to Penygadair was a popular route, but now the zigzag path up the upper screes is so loose and eroded I cannot recommend it beyond the shores of Llyn y Gadair (see Route C10).

RIDGE ROUTES

Cyfrwy

Distance: ½ mile/800m
Height gain: 130ft/40m
Time: 20 minutes

Descend westwards from the summit then take the right fork – the Pony Path – which traces the rim of Llyn y Gadair's cwm. Where the Pony Path slants left over the shoulder of Cyfrwy, leave it to continue by the edge and make a direct ascent across stony ground to the summit.

Mynydd Moel

Distance: 1¼ miles/2km
Height gain: 245ft/75m
Time: ¾ hour

This is a simple but steepish descent north of west over boulders at first, which then becomes a fine stride across firm terrain of rock and grass. You can either follow the edge or a parallel path to the right. There's a steady but easy climb to Mynydd Moel's summit.

Mynydd Pencoed

Distance: 1½ miles/2.5km (west summit);
    ¾ mile/1.2km (east summit)
Height gain: 295ft/90m
Time: 1 hour (west summit); ½ hour (east summit)

Descend south-west through rocky terrain making sure to avoid the Pony Path route

Above: The final climb of Routes C14/15 to Penygadair from Cwm Cau.

which forks off to the right along Penygadair's northern edge. Eventually the path nears the edge of Cwm Cau. From the col between the two mountains the path climbs more rocky terrain. Halfway up there's a fork in the path where you take the left fork, which stays close to the edge above Craig Cau. This will lead to the higher east summit, a stony top with a fence and ladder stile on top.

The right fork is a shortcut to the west summit and follows a line parallel with but above a fence on the right. It joins the ridge halfway between the summits. Turn right and follow the fence to the west summit.

Tyrau Mawr

Distance: 2¼ miles/3.6km
Height gain: 330ft/100m
Time: 1½ hours

Descend WSW along the cairned Pony Path, which soon after leaving the summit forks right and hugs the northern edge above Llyn y Gadair, then veers left along the southern breast of Cyfrwy. It descends to Rhiw Gwredydd, where you cross a ladder stile and climb a narrower fence-side path up grassy slopes. It passes the cairn and rocks of Carnedd Lwyd before coming to the grass and bilberry summit of Tyrau Mawr.

The trouble with Mynydd Moel is that it is too close to Penygadair to be considered as anything other than a peak-bagger's tick in the logbook. It's also hampered by a name that means 'featureless mountain.' How unfair!

Seen from Dolgellau, Mynydd Moel is the dominant peak of the Cadair Idris range, a proud cone-like summit seemingly rising higher than the others. Unlike many of Cadair's other peaks, Mynydd Moel has rock-faces on both the Mawddach and southern sides, though they're more severe in the north. The summit has a good-sized windshelter not far from the precipices and a huge stony gully plummeting into anonymous slopes interspersed with crag, heather and a tiny tarn, Llyn Arran.

Mynydd Moel's ridge declines gently and uneventfully north-eastwards towards the green pastures of Dolgellau, but the mountain has one last trump card to play. Beyond an unsuspecting little summit knoll, the ground suddenly falls away in the dark dramatic cliffs of Gau Graig. On closer inspection Gau Graig's east face is split into two. The most prominent is the delightful

north-east ridge, where heather intermingles with crusty crags, while sparse wind-warped rowans and thorn trees hang precariously from ledges.

A much shorter and steeper spur is thrown out from Gau Graig's summit. Between the two there's a dark, unnamed and unfrequented hollow.

Opposite: The northern crags of Mynydd Moel.
Above right: Gau Craig from the bridleway.

Route C16
Gau Graig and the North-East Ridge
A fascinating but little-used route
Start: Lay-by car park in Cwm Rhwyddfor
  (GR: SH 753136)
Distance: 3 miles/5km
Height gain: 2100ft/640m
Time: 2 hours

The path begins over a ladder stile across the road from the car park. Turn left following a little path parallel to the road before going over the next ladder stile. Follow the road's grass verge over the pass to another ladder stile, where a signed bridleway begins. It contours around the lower slopes of Mynydd Gwerngraig. A stream comes down from the left. This should be crossed to reach the ladder stile on the other side before continuing up the hillside. Now Gau Graig is in full view to the left. Note the white post ahead, but stay close to an old enclosed track on the right, now choked with rushes and thickets.

On reaching the crumbled wall to the right of the white post, leave the bridleway and climb half-left (west) to cross a ladder stile in a drystone wall (GR 753151). Keep well to the south of the oak woods further along the bridleway. Now a delightful path climbs Gau Graig's north-east ridge. It twists and turns among crags interspersed with heather and bilberry before reaching Gau Graig's summit.

The summit cairn, ringed by a broken down wall, lies the other side of the fence and you have to go a short way past it to gain the two stiles allowing you access. Although Mynydd Moel blocks views to the west, those to the north and east are fascinating. The north-east ridge with its little bluffs and cliffs leads your gaze down to the slate roofs of Dolgellau. Beyond it the Rhinog mountains line up, each one offset just enough to let you see its summit.

Return to the two stiles and continue either side of the ridge fence across terrain which is marshy in places. Mynydd Moel's buttresses

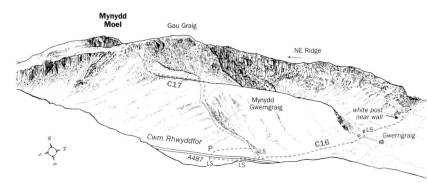

68

Above: Gau Graig from just beyond the early stream-crossing on Route C16.

always look powerful and impressive as you amble along this extensive flat ridge, which is punctuated by a couple of rocky knolls. The fence eventually parts company with the path and plummets to the tarn Llyn Aran and soon the ground gets steeper, firmer and rockier as you climb along the northern edge of the final slopes to the summit.

Route C17

Mynydd Gwerngraig and Gau Graig

A tough climb without the elegance of
Route C16

Start: Lay-by car park in Cwm Rhwyddfor
(GR: SH 753136)

Distance: 2½ miles/4km

Height gain: 2035ft/620m

Time: 1¼ hours

Before you start this route I must admit that
it's only here for completeness. It's tough,
inferior in every way to Route C16, and the
path is quite loose on the final climb to Gau
Graig.

Climb north-east from the back of the car
park up to the fence on Mynydd Gwerngraig's ridge. A narrow path now climbs by
the fence on steep grassy slopes. The path
levels off in the mid stages and Gau Graig's
south-western crags appear directly ahead.
The route climbs more steeply again towards
the screes below these crags. On reaching the
bottom of the screes the path veers right,
away from the fence. At the base of the crags
a loose winding path climbs a shallow gully
before returning to the fence near the rim of
the ridge.

You could cut a corner here and head west
towards the main ridge fence, but the ground
is rough and marshy in places and it is easier
to head north-west alongside the fence which
has guided you thus far, to the summit of Gau
Graig. The summit cairn lies a short way
north-east and is well worth the detour to
see the fine knobbly crags and heather of the
narrowing north-east ridge.

After returning to the main ridge path,
follow it across what is sometimes marshy
terrain, with Mynydd Moel's impressive crags
directly ahead. The ground steepens and the
path climbs among the crags to the summit.
The fence eventually parts company with the
path and plummets to the tarn called Llyn
Aran. Soon the ground gets steeper, firmer
and rockier as you climb the final slopes to
the summit.

Above: The upper part of Route C17, showing the grassy top of Mynydd Gwerngraig and the rocky climb to Cadair's north-east ridge.

Route C18

Minffordd and the south slopes

A direct line spoiled a little by a steep,
*   eroded middle section*

Start: Minffordd car park (GR: SH 732116)

Distance: 2 miles/3 km

Height gain: 2525ft/770m

Time: 1½ hours

From the toilet block at the back of Min-ffordd's car park follow the Cadair Idris signs of the Minffordd Path. The well-defined route takes you through an avenue of trees, past the National Trust house at Ystradgwyn. A meandering path climbs in man-made steps through oak woods into the mouth of Cwm

Cau. Here, at the top edge of the trees, you leave the Minffordd Path and cross Nant Cadair. A narrow path now takes you north-west up the grassy north side of Moelfryn.

After going over a ladder stile straddling a wall, turn left and follow the wall on a loose stony path. Beyond a second ladder stile the path becomes steeper and horribly eroded with loose stones everywhere.

You can follow Route C15 to the ridge by turning left over the third stile and climbing along the eastern edge of Cwm Cau before turning right up the final slopes of Mynydd Moel. However, if you are in a hurry, it is quicker and more logical to continue by the fence to the summit.

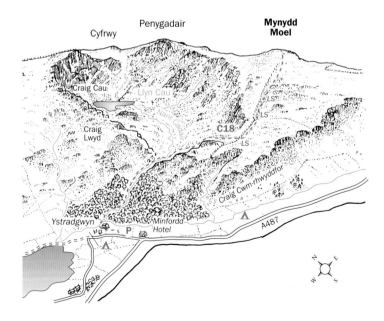

Other route options

I looked at routes to Mynydd Moel from Llyn Arran but they appear very difficult and rough, even when taking the lower cliffs to the east.

RIDGE ROUTES

Penygadair

Distance: 1¼ miles/2km
Height gain: 330ft/100m
Time: ¾ hour

Penygadair looks very distinctive from Mynydd Moel, with a Blencathra-like saddle of rock. Perhaps *this* is the seat of Idris? The route is easy-paced and firm. Walkers can follow the very edge or take the more prominent southerly path. The ground steepens and becomes bouldery as the path climbs on to Penygadair's summit ridge. First you come to the stone refuge shelter just to the north-east of the pile of stones marking the summit.

Gau Graig

Distance: 1¼ miles /2km
Height gain: 100ft/30m
Time: ¾ hour

This mostly downhill route starts on a good path, quite close to the spectacularly rocky northern edge. At the bottom of the steep rise the path runs alongside a fence, which will take you most of the way. The terrain is a little marshy in places but not unacceptably so. At a junction of fences (GR 743140) turn right, then go left over a step stile to reach the wall-ringed Bronze Age cairn marking Gau Graig's summit.

Below: The descent of Mynydd Moel's southern slopes with Llyn Mwyngil below.

Above: Gau Graig seen from its north-east ridge.

GAU GRAIG

Cadair Idris ends in the east with magnificent Gau Graig overlooking the fields above the Wnion valley. Seen from the Cross Foxes Inn this end looks like one impressive rock-face, but closer inspection reveals that the crags are in a narrow hollow bound by a stubby rock spur and the gnarled finger of the north-east ridge. This is the clue to the real name, which probably should be Cau Crag, the crag of the hollow ('gau' means false).

I've not included any routes to Gau Graig as such, as it's just the arm of Mynydd Moel and all routes would naturally continue at least as far as that peak. Thus the two routes up Gau Graig, C16 and C17, appear below among the routes to Mynydd Moel. However, it is a fine viewpoint and the view of it is so well known that it must rank a mention. The summit lies at the north-east end of the main ridge overlooking the previously mentioned stubby rock spur and the hollow. It is topped with a small Bronze Age cairn ringed with a drystone-walled enclosure.

Mynydd Pencoed has an identity crisis. In various walkers' books it's been called both Craig Cwm Amarch and Craig Cau, names referring only to the crags overlooking cwms on the south and east side of the mountain. Meanwhile the OS Explorer map attaches the hill's actual name to its low and lumpy south-western spur.

Seen from the west, Mynydd Pencoed is merely a rounded grassy hump – a big hump, but nothing to get excited about. Seen from the lakeside at Tal-y-llyn, the peak offers previews of its grandeur, with the slaty Cwm Amarch peeping over a hanging valley, some conifers and some waterfalls. But Mynydd Pencoed comes into its own when viewed from Cwm Cau. Here the cliffs of Craig Cau burst from tarn to summit in a great dark triangle of rock divided by two gullies and the towering Pencoed Pillar.

There are two summits. The more popular east summit lies on the Minffordd Path. It's a rocky top straddled by a fence, but there's no trig point or large cairn, only a ladder stile. Penygadair and Mynydd Moel restrict views to the north, otherwise there are fine panoramas of Cwm Cau, Tal-y-llyn and the lush Pennant Valley.

The west summit is slightly lower and off the usual Cadair Idris routes, but somehow it seems more like a top should be, with its own separate ridge known as Daear Fawr. There are numerous grassy corners for a peaceful picnic, with views over the lonely hanging valley of Cwm Amarch, high above the glimmering lake at Tal-y-llyn. The best ascent route to Mynydd Pencoed has already been described in Route C13 to Penygadair. To reach the west summit it's just a short detour left along the fence-line.

Opposite: The cliffs of Craig Cau and Mynydd Pencoed's east summit.
Right: Mynydd Pencoed's west slopes above the Afon Cadair.

Route C19
Pentre and Cwm Amarch

*A very tough walk with steep pathless
  ascents. Better as a descent route*
Start: Minffordd car park (GR: SH 732116)
Distance: 3 miles/4.8km
Height gain: 2360ft/720m
Time: 2–2½ hours

The walk starts in easy fashion on the valley
floor. After going back through the car park
entrance, turn right along the B4405 road
towards Llyn Mwyngil. At the sharp left-hand
bend leave the road for a farm lane, which
maintains your direction along the foot of the
mountain slopes and a short distance from
the shores of the lake.

Beneath Pentre Farm you leave the lane for
a track on the right, which lies beyond a gate.
Keep to the right of the farmhouse, aiming for
a ladder stile at the edge of a wood. Climb
along a slaty path to emerge at the bottom of
a grass cwm with a stream to the left. Here
the path marked on the map all but dies out
and the going gets very tough.

Follow the stream-side for a short way then
take one of the grassy channels up the hillside
on the right. Where this gives out, climb the
pathless slopes in a north-west direction,
keeping the waterfalls and the surrounding
rock-faces well to the left. Eventually the
ground levels out as you reach the lip of Cwm
Amarch. There are several easy places to ford
the stream here.

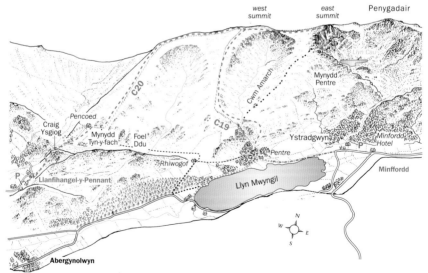

Beyond the crossing, head for the west spur, where a fence leads up more very steep grassy slopes. Keep an eye on the view back; it may help you bear the strain of the climb. It's dominated by Llyn Mwyngil and the whitewashed Ty'n y Cornel Hotel, which is dwarfed by the soaring scree slopes of Graig Goch.

The gradient eases beyond a small pool, and the increasingly spectacular scenery takes the sting out of the final slopes to the ridge. Here you turn right and follow the fence, first to the west summit, then to the rockier east one.

Descent

From the west summit, follow the fence-line south, down the spur on the west side of Cwm Amarch, to the lower regions of the cwm. Leave the spur when gradients on the left ease to allow a beeline across the rushy cwm to the east side. You should be able to pick up a faint track, which descends well to the left of the waterfalls before fading out on the grassy slopes of Mynydd Pentre. From here zigzag down the steep grassy slopes, aiming for the forest corner at the bottom of the cwm. Here you go over a stile and follow the slaty path past Pentre Farm out on to the lane by the lake. Turn left here back to the car park.

Route C20
Llanfihangel and Pencoed

Another steep climb, better as a descent
Start: Llanfihangel-y-pennant
  (GR: SH 672088)
Distance: 3½ miles/5.5km
Height gain: 2560ft/780m
Time: 2 hours

Turn right out of the car park and follow the lane north up the valley. Before reaching the houses of Tynyfach watch out for a stile on the right, which marks the start of the clear track to be followed. On nearing those houses you come to a stony track at the apex of a sharp bend – take the waymarked right-hand course, which rakes across the lower slopes of Mynydd Tyn-y-fach. Stay with the main track, ignoring the right fork.

Next the track contours around the base of Craig Ysgiog. Just beyond the crossing of Nant Pencoed leave the track and climb a zigzagging path up the bracken-clad fields. Soon you'll see a ruin above you – aim for this to find the gap in the wall at GR 683109. Continue the climb south-eastwards to locate the ladder stile and gate by the stone buildings of Pencoed. From the old farmhouse follow the path to the right and go over the step stile into open country.

Now climb the steep grassy slopes of Mynydd Pencoed to gain the ridge. The going is easy along Daear Fawr, with a fence to guide you to the summit, and it's worth detouring to the south rim to see the views down Cwm Amarch.

Descent

This is more straightforward in descent. Head down south-west and when the buildings of Pencoed come into view aim to the left of them to locate the stile. Descend south-west and through a gap in a wall, passing some ruins before following a zigzag path to the stony farm track, where you turn left, over the stream and back to Llanfihangel-y-Pennant.

Other route options

The obvious one is to follow the Minffordd Path (Route C13) to the top of Craig Cau (791m spot height), then turn off westwards by the ridge fence to Pencoed's west summit. You could also follow Route C18 to Pentre Farm but turn left behind the old farm to take the path to Rhiwogof farm (see Route C23 below).

A zigzag track continues into the valley of Nant Pencoed, where you could either turn right to climb to Graig Ddu where the steep spur soon meets Route C18 again, or you can continue towards Pencoed (an old farm-house, not currently occupied) and take the steep grassy spur used in Route C19.

RIDGE ROUTE

Penygadair

Distance: 1½ miles/2.5km (west summit);
　　¾ mile/1.2km (east summit)
Height gain: 850ft/260m (west summit);
　　690ft/210m (east summit)
Time: 1 hour (west summit);
　　1¼ hour (east summit)

Follow the fence from the west summit to the east. Here turn left and go over the ladder stile. You can either follow the edge of Cwm Cau (which is dangerous when there's snow and ice about), or trace the well-defined path down to the col. From here a cairned route leads over boulders to Penygadair's summit trig point.

Opposite: Descending the ridge flanking Cwm Amarch towards Tal-y-llyn.

From almost anywhere in the Dysynni Valley, Craig yr Aderyn cuts a fine figure, with precipitous cliffs rising straight out of the lush riverside fields to a rocky dome. Here, you'll be able to see the crumbling walls of an Iron Age fort. What a view of the enemy these warriors must have had – on one side down the emerald Dysynni Valley to the sea at Cardigan Bay; on the other, Cadair Idris, whose more gentle rounded contours look as though they might have been borrowed from a South Lakeland landscape.

In reality the highest peak lies to the south of the popular one, but lacking those spectacular drops, it gets rather neglected. To the north-east Craig yr Aderyn throws out a splendid rocky spur declining to Llanllwyda.

In times gone by the valley's fields were under water, a wide sea estuary cutting deep into Cadair country. Craig yr Aderyn formed impressive sea cliffs, which would have echoed to the sounds of gulls and cormorants. Centuries after the sea has receded some four miles, the cormorants still come to nest in their only European inland breeding site – something not lost on Charles Darwin,

Opposite: Craig yr Aderyn towers above the flat fields of the Dysynni Valley.
Right: On the summit of Craig yr Aderyn.

who spent many hours here studying their movements. The site is also an important breeding and roosting ground for the chough, a bright red-legged and beaked member of the crow family.

Looking at the map there are no marked public footpaths to Craig yr Aderyn, but they do exist on the ground. Considering it has such fierce faces, Bird Rock offers very easy short walks. Though climbers attack the cliffs full on, walkers can sneak round the back and follow a swathe of short-cropped grass, rather like the limestone dales of Yorkshire, right to the top. There's even a viewing seat halfway up!

Route C21
Llanllwyda

The quick and logical way, it's also the best

Start: Limited roadside parking at Llanllwyda (GR: SH 651076)

Distance: 1¼ miles/2 km

Height gain: 855ft/260m

Time: ½–¾ hour

The bridleway begins opposite the campsite at Llanllwyda farm at a place marked by some picnic tables. After a short way it joins a wide track climbing beneath Craig yr Aderyn's north-east spur.

The route to the summit, not marked on current maps, leaves the track on the approach to a left-hand bend. Just a faded path in the grass at first, the route becomes more pronounced as it gains height. Halfway up there's a fork in the path. The right fork leads to the lower but more popular north summit. Follow it to a grassy col then turn right along a cairned path over rocks to the fort on the summit.

If you want to tackle the higher south summit then take the left fork, which climbs to the foot of the crags. A narrow path then rakes up the steep north-west face above rashes of boulders. It fades on a grassy spur, but from here you simply turn left and climb to the huge hollowed-out cairn on the summit. Return by the same route.

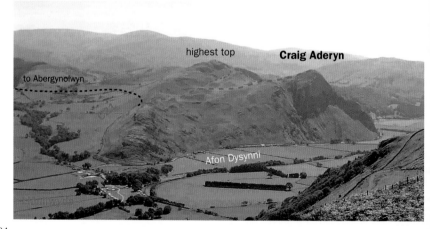

to Abergynolwyn

highest top

Craig Aderyn

Afon Dysynni

Above: The view to Cadair Idris from Craig yr Aderyn.

FOEL DDU

Foel Ddu, the bare black hill, is connected to Mynydd Pencoed on Cadair Idris by the slenderest of low ridges, which is almost severed by the desolate marshy valley of Nant Pencoed. The hill is craggy and rugged, and along with neighbour Mynydd Ty'n-y-fach forms a wishbone-shaped hill overlooking Llyn Mwyngil at Tal-y-llyn, and the valleys of the Dysynni and Afon Cadair. The southern slopes above the Dysynni are cloaked with woodland, mostly conifers, but with enough broadleaved trees to make things interesting on routes to the heathery ridge.

In the valley of Nant y Eira, which drains Foel Ddu's western slopes, there are some pleasant waterfalls. The stream tumbles further to Llanfihangel-y-pennant, where there is an attractive stone-built chapel dating back to the twelfth century. These days it's dedicated to Mary Jones, a poor eighteenth-century weaver's daughter, who, as a 16-year-old with no shoes to wear, decided she wanted her own bible and made her way across the hills to Bala (probably over the shoulder of Foel Ddu), some 30 miles/48 km away. Mary's cottage, Tyn-y-ddol, and a monument

Left: The west ridge of Foel Ddu.

to her can be found a short way north up the road, as can the ancient rock-perched fortress of Castell y Bere, long occupied by the Princes of Wales.

Below: The Mary Jones monument, Llanfihangel-y-pennant.

Route C22
Abergynolwyn
The easiest way to the summit

Start: Pandy Square, Abergynolwyn
  (GR: SH 678069)

Distance: 3 miles/5.2 km

Height gain: 1445ft/440m

Time: 1½–2 hours

Cross the road to the Railway Inn and take the lane signposted to Llanfihangel. At the far side of the bridge spanning the Dysynni river, turn right through a kissing gate and trace the north banks to a step stile in a fence. Beyond this you turn left and climb to a country lane. Turn right along the lane. At its junction with the B4405 turn left over a ladder stile, and climb north-west across a field. Continue over two more stiles to a woodland path. Climb along this to reach a forestry track near the top edge of the woods.

Turn left along the track, which soon veers right to a gate and adjacent stile giving entry into a large field. To the right you'll see a track crossing to the far (right) side of the field but it's not strictly legal until it enters the access land. Instead follow the wall on the left (on the right of way) until you come to a crumbling cross-wall. Now turn right and follow the wall to reach the previously mentioned track. The splendidly firm grass track meanders up a broad grassy ridge with the crags of Mynydd Tyn-y-fach ahead and the ground on the left falling away to the fields of Llanfihangel-y-pennant.

The track ends but the terrain is quite good. Just head north-eastwards along the ridge with the angular peak of Foel Ddu now in view ahead. Go through a gate in a wall, which comes in from the right before guiding the route ahead towards those peaks. The grassy swathe to the right of the wall gives the easiest passage to the summit.

It's probably worth a brief diversion here to a crest on the right for fine views of Llyn Mwyngil and the cliffs of Graig Goch. Make your way back to the grassy swathe and follow it upwards. Near the top you'll see an obvious narrow grassy ribbon through heather and crag on the left. Climb up this to reach a fence and follow this left to the summit.

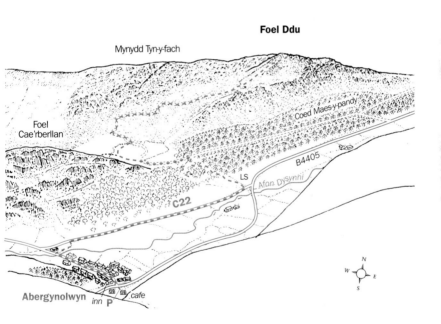

89

Route C23
Minffordd

A very pleasant lakeside panorama path
Start: Minffordd car park (GR: SH 732116)
Distance: 3 miles/5 km
Height gain: 1280ft/390m
Time: 1½–2 hours

Out of the car park, turn right along the B4405 road, passing the campsite on the way to the first left-hand bend. Here leave the road for a farm lane heading towards Llyn Mwyngil. After passing through lakeside pastures with fine views of Graig Goch and the picturesque inns of Tal-y-llyn, you come to Pentre, an old farmhouse in a slightly raised position on the right. Turn right along the track to the farm before passing behind the main house towards the trees surrounding Cwm Amarch's stream.

A footbridge spans the stream and the path climbs the far banks to pass through a gate into a large field beneath the rock-fringed Graig Ddu. The current map shows a zigzag right of way climbing the hill, but in reality this doesn't exist. Instead climb north-west up the steep slopes passing a waymarker post halfway up. The marked track begins at the top edge of the woods at GR 714104. It's a glorious track with views of the lake below you and to the falls of Cwm Amarch above.

When you reach Rhiwogof farm double back right on another track winding up to the

Left: Tal-y-llyn and Llyn Mwyngil from the slopes of Foel Ddu.

pass between Mynydd Pencoed and Foel Ddu. After a big loop the track comes to a gate and a ladder stile at GR 707103. Just beyond this you'll see a faint path on the left, which heads south across rough grassland to the foot of Foel Ddu to join the faint right of way from Pencoed, which runs alongside a fence on the left at first. Stay with the fence as it angles up towards Foel Ddu's north-east ridge. Although pathless the route has no real problems, for there's a convenient gap in a cross-wall as you near the ridge.

The terrain becomes more rocky once on the ridge. A wall soon veers off across the precipitous craggy southern slopes, but you must stay near the crest all the way to the summit.

Descent

Follow the crest eastwards at first, then ENE, ignoring what may seem like a ridge wall (it soon traverses the steep south-east flanks). Where there's a meeting of walls (GR 702097) look for a gap in the wall on the left and, once through it, descend by a fence declining to the col between Foel Ddu and Mynydd Pencoed, whose shaley crags are quite impressive and domineering. You'll see a prominent track ahead and the route will use this to get down to the lakeside.

Once at the col follow the fence as it veers left. Soon you'll see a faint path heading north to meet this track. Follow the track right as it winds down the hillside to Rhiwogof farm. Double back left on a waymarked path at the farmhouse. The new track traverses

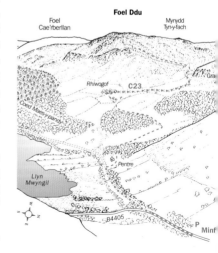

high fields but ends at the top of some woods (GR 714104).

Don't look for the right-of-way zigzags – they don't exist – but descend south-east down the steep, pastured hillside. A gate and stile allow entry into the woods surrounding Cwm Amarch's stream. Cross the footbridge and go behind Pentre's farmhouse. A track leads to the farm lane, which leads to the left across lakeside fields towards Minffordd.

Other route options

The final climb on Route C22 could also be accessed from the Cadair Valley at Llanfi-hangel-y-pennant on a fine path through woods and past waterfalls. In another route from the same hamlet, a track from the back of Ty'n-y-ddol rakes up north-east across the lower slopes of Mynydd Tyn-y-fach. It fades somewhat on reaching the little gorge of an unnamed stream (GR 681099) but continues as a faint path, almost reaching the summit of Craig Ysgiog. From here you can traverse craggy slopes on to Mynydd Ty'n-y-fach and finally Foel Ddu.

Opposite: The footbridge behind Pentre.
Below: Foel Ddu's east ridge from Llyn Mwyngil.

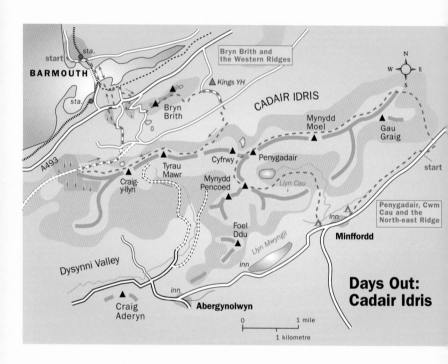

Bryn Brith and
the Western Ridges

↑ Kings YH

CADAIR IDRIS

BARMOUTH

start

sta.

sta.

Bryn
Brith

Mynydd
Moel

Gau
Graig

start

A493

Tyrau
Mawr

Cyfrwy

Penygadair

Craig-
y-llyn

Mynydd
Pencoed

Llyn Cau

inn

Penygadair, Cwm
Cau and the
North-east Ridge

Foel
Ddu

Llyn Mwyngil

Minffordd

Dysynni Valley

inn

inn

Craig
Aderyn

Abergynolwyn

0   1 mile

1 kilometre

N
W   E
S

**Days Out:
Cadair Idris**

Opposite: Bryn Brith (left) and Tyrau Mawr (right) from across the Mawddach Estuary.

Bryn Brith and the Western Ridges

A very big and beautiful day out

Start: Barmouth Promenade (GR: SH 613155)
Distance: 13 miles/21 km
Height gain: 3770ft/1150m
Time: 8–9 hours

I've already eulogised about how good Cadair looks from across the Mawddach, and about its superb location near to the coast. Well, this splendid day out will show the full experience. We'll start from sea level, across Wordsworth's 'sublime estuary', and walk to the high ridges the purists' way. On this epic journey, you'll experience walks through the woods, past waterfalls and magnificent lakes and tarns; and you'll get to grips with a little rock scramble and stride out along easy grassy ridges.

You don't have to walk on water – just pay the nice man a small toll and he'll let you walk across the mile-long footway which runs alongside the magnificent Victorian railway bridge built in 1867. Tyrau Mawr is the dominant peak at first, but as you cross it sinks beneath the lower wooded foothills.

If the tide is out you'll be able to follow the embankment eastwards to the north side of the wooded knoll of Fegla Fawr. If not, continue southwards towards Morfa Mawddach

railway station. Just before reaching it you'll see a track doubling back left towards the same knoll. The right of way goes behind the terrace of red brick houses, Mawddach Crescent, before continuing for a short way along the estuary bank before rejoining the embankment route at the north side of Fegla Fawr.

At a gate turn right and follow a firm grassy path traversing marshland. This path meets the tree-lined trackbed of the old Dolgellau railway, which you follow to the left. Where the track crosses the little estuary of the Arthog river, leave it and turn right along a tarmac lane past a small car park. After going over a ladder stile on the left you follow a grass embankment by the river to reach the main road at St Catherine's Church. Opposite the church a footpath begins with some steps into woodland. The well-waymarked path climbs to cross the apex of a lane before continuing uphill through more woodland in the gorge of the Arthog, a bustling white-water river which is, in some places, far below the path.

Over a ladder stile at the top edge of the woods turn left and go over a slabbed bridge where a grass path leads to a farm track. Where the farm track veers right leave it to maintain direction by following a drystone wall on the left. The path across these high fields above the Mawddach is well way-marked, making detailed route description unnecessary. The imposing rock you can see ahead is Bryn Brith. There's a short stretch of walled track on the left to go down before turning right across a field to a ladder stile. More waymarks lead the route north-east-wards across bouldery low hillside before dropping down to reach a lane, where you turn right.

After the lane weaves through the rocks to the top of a pass, the lakes of Cregennen come into view, with Tyrau Mawr's rock and scree slopes forming the perfect backdrop. Not far beyond this point turn left along a clear footpath traversing rushy moorland to the north of the larger, northern lake.

Beyond a ladder stile over a fence leave the main path for a narrow left fork heading directly for Bryn Brith. The entertaining path scrambles over rock and heather – you'll need to use your hands in a couple of places – before reaching the ancient summit hill fort. There's a memorable view across Cregennen to Tyrau Mawr and Craig-y-llyn – in summer it's very green, in winter the russets of heather and bracken add a new dimension to a more brooding scene.

From the hill fort, continue north-east-wards along the undulating rocky ridge, then descend into a large grassy hollow where you can continue the descent to the right (south-east) along a narrow path down to the path running along the base of the southern slopes (GR 670151). Turn left along this, passing through a shallow dry valley.

The path turns left on the approach to Ty'n-llidiart, goes through a gate, and turns half-right to pass through a gateway close to the cottage. (The small plantation shown on the map is no longer there.) Now below the cottage, you turn left along the edge of a field, heading east along a farm track, which meets a stream and follows it out to the road south-west of Kings Youth Hostel. Turn right on this, following it uphill to the T-junction with Cader Road.

After going left along this for 300 yards/m, watch out for an unsigned path on the right – it's opposite the signed one on the left to Tynyceunant. Through a gate a zigzag sunken grass track takes you up the hillslopes. After going through a narrow gap in a cross-wall the path heads SSE to a stream, which it follows to a ladder stile near a wall corner. Beyond this you meet the Pony Path (Route C11), a heavily engineered slab path which zigzags to the top of the pass, Rhiw Gwredydd.

You now turn your attentions to the west, where one of Wales's best ridge routes awaits you. Over a ladder stile the path climbs steadily up grassy slopes, passing the rocks and large cairn of Carnedd Lwyd. So far you've been well away from the edge, but as you approach Tyrau Mawr's summit a ladder stile in the fence allows you to explore a more exciting edge path – there are some fine gullies and weirdly shaped rocky tors hereabouts.

The path down the other side is quite steep, but without complication, then it's more of the same up to Craig-y-llyn. This is a slightly less spectacular peak, but one with its own tarn, Llyn Cyri (not visited on this route).

A faint path descends the east slopes, passing the cairn at Twll yr Ogof before reaching a col. Now you're on the edge of some of the highest cattle pastures in Wales; they're the upper reaches of Nant Caw's farmland. The main ridge here arcs north, though there's a subsidiary ridge over to Trawsfynydd in the west. Follow the north side of the fence, keeping to the right of the forestry plantations, which all but engulf Braich Ddu.

At Braich Ddu's summit the ridge turns west again and you descend, still by the plantation's edge, to a high stony track where you turn right. Follow this downhill, past a memorial to the crew of a World War II Flying Fortress, which crashed here in 1945. Take the left fork to descend to the junction of tarred lanes at GR 648133. Ignoring the lane on the left (to Cyfannedd), descend northwards along the lane ahead, passing the farming complex at Cregennen (not the lakes).

Just beyond a sharp right-hand bend, take the stony track on the left past the cottage of Merddyn. A path leaves the footpath on the left and descends into woodland, passing beneath the spoil of an old quarry before descending to the main Dolgellau road by Arthog's village hall. Turn right along the road, then left along a signed path leading the route back to the old railway trackbed. Follow this back to Morfa Mawddach station before taking the lane back to the bridge and the outward route from Barmouth.

Overleaf: View from Tyrau Mawr across the lakes of Cregennen to Barmouth and the Mawddach Estuary.

Penygadair, Cwm Cau and the North-east Ridge

See all the exciting crags of Cadair's big peaks in one walk

Start: Lay-by car park in Cwm Rhwyddfor (GR: SH 753136)

Distance: 8¼ miles/14km

Height gain: 3250ft/990m

Time: 5–6 hours

The path proper begins just over the top of the pass towards Dolgellau. To save much of the road-walking go over the ladder stile opposite the car park and turn left on grassland beneath the cliffs of Craig y Llam. Go over another stile and you're back on the road but there's not that far to go. Another ladder stile marks the start of the bridleway, which rounds the slopes of Mynydd Gwerngraig.

After fording a stream on the right go over a ladder stile and follow the continuing path up the hillside staying close to an old enclosed track, now choked with rushes and thickets. Gau Graig is now in full view to the left. Note the white post near the tumble-down cross-wall ahead. On reaching the wall and post, leave the bridleway and climb half-left (west) to locate and cross a ladder stile in a drystone wall.

A delightful path climbs Gau Graig's north-east ridge among crags and heather. All too quickly the ridge ends at Gau Graig's summit. The terrain is a bit soggy in places but this is compensated for by the sight of Mynydd Moel and its powerful northern buttresses ahead.

As the ground gets steeper towards that summit it also gets firmer and rockier. The highlight of Mynydd Moel is the huge stony

Left: Gau Graig's North-East Ridge.

Above: Cwm Cau from edge of Penygadair.

gully plummeting to an anonymous and seldom-trod complex of low craggy knolls. Here among the stones and heather you'll spot a tiny tarn, Llyn Aran.

Now Penygadair lies at the far end of a stony ridge. You can follow the edge on the right (which can be dangerous if there's a snow cornice in winter) or take the more prominent ridge path. The ground steepens and becomes broken and stony as the path tackles Penygadair's final slopes. There's a stone refuge shelter for those caught out by bad weather. By going to the edges you'll be able to see two views down spectacular lake-filled corries, Cwm Cau and Cwm y Gadair.

The route will now round the rim of Cwm Cau to the summit of Mynydd Pencoed. Be careful to locate the start of the path descending south-west away from those northern cliffs as it's easy to mistake the Minffordd Path

for the cairned, right-fork Pony Path, which follows the rim of Llyn y Gadair's cwm.

Halfway up the ascent to Mynydd Pencoed, ignore the path forking right above the line of a fence, but stay by the main fence to reach the ladder stile marking the east summit. Once over this follow the well-defined path descending south-east above the gullies surrounding Pencoed Pillar. The path eventually clambers down left into Cwm Cau before veering right into oak woods. Here a stepped path descends past the car park at Minffordd and out on to the road. Follow this left past the Minffordd Hotel, where you will have earned one of their good bar meals.

After turning left along the main Dolgellau road, turn left again along the bridleway track up Bwlch llyn Bach, passing the campsite then follow a stream back to the road just short of the lay-by car park.

The Dyfi and Tarren Hills

Dinas Mawddwy

⑲

⑮ ⑰

⑯

inn

Cribin Fawr ▲

A470 Maesglase ▲

1

Waun-oer ▲

Craig Portas ▲

Foel Dinas ▲

⑳

㉒

CADAIR IDRIS

Minffordd

⛰

inn

Mynydd Fron-fraith ▲

DYFI HILLS

Llyn Mwyngil

② ⑥

⑦ ⑧

⑨

inn

①

Graig Goch ▲

㉑

⑱

Aberllefenni

Corris

Abergynolwyn *inn*

⑩

sta. *sta.*

Dolgoch

④

Pantperthog

Afon Dyfi

sta.

A470

Bryncrug

⑫

sta.

Tarren y Gesail ▲

Tarrenhendre ▲

Mynydd Rhyd-galed ▲

main line railway

Talyllyn railway

Tarren Cwm-ffernol ▲

Trum Gelli ▲

TARREN HILLS

③

sta.

⑪ ⑤

Pennal

Cwrt

⑬

MACHYNLLETH

0   1 mile
1 kilometre

N
W ◆ E
S

2. The Dyfi and Tarren Hills

South of Cadair Idris the hard rock world of the Ordovician era transforms into the softer, rounded Silurian hills. Geologically and geographically the Tarren and Dyfi hills are on the borderline: they're still proper mountains but the crags are more sparse and often partially vegetated.

THE PEAKS

Main Tops	height	
Maesglase	2218ft	676m
Waun-oer	2197ft	670m
Tarren y Gesail	2187ft	667m
Cribin Fawr	2161ft	659m
Tarrenhendre	2079ft	634m
Craig Portas	1984ft	605m
Graig Goch	1922ft	586m
Tarren Cwm-ffernol	1804ft	550m
Trum Gelli	1754ft	535m
Mynydd Ffron-fraith	1685ft	514m
Mynydd Cwm-yr-eglwys	1669ft	509m
Foel Dinas	1567ft	478m
Mynydd Rhyd-galed	1558ft	475m

The Tarren hills rise from the pleasant little fishing village of Aberdyfi and the Victorian resort of Tywyn on the shores of Cardigan Bay. Their 12-mile/19km ridge reaches the 2000ft mark at just two points, Tarrenhendre and Tarren y Gesail. In the north and south two rivers, the Dysynni and the Dyfi, border the Tarrens. The former separates them from the more glamorous Cadair Idris, while the latter marks the boundaries of Machynlleth and Mid Wales.

Beyond Tarren y Gesail the range gets engulfed in mass forestry and declines into sullen anonymity around the slate village of Corris. 'Well, we know where to come to get our Christmas trees,' my nephew Roy grumbled as he slogged up the steep hill out of Abergynolwyn and into Cwm Gwernol. The dark spruce trees were streaming with excess moisture and echoing to the mews of a kestrel soaring over Tarrenhendre's half-moon shaped crags, which sulked in the still, dismal light.

Halfway down the valley are the massive quarries of Bryn Eglwys (church hill). The slate quarries were closed down in 1947 after a very successful century and a half of operation. The slate was transported by the Talyllyn narrow-gauge railway down to Tywyn, from where it was shipped to all parts of the world. There's a large, fairly

103

Above: Although the valley of Nant Gwernol in the Tarren Hills is filled with conifers it also has fine deciduous woodland and a bounding stream.

intact, pulley house on the hillside above (the Beaunewydd Incline) and great piles of slate waste rise up from the streambed.

We'd been hearing the sound of thundering water for some time. The source turned out to be two of the valley's tributary streams plunging 50ft/15m into the murky depths of a gigantic collapsed cavern. Through the clearing mist I caught sight of a monkey-puzzle tree among the ghostly ruins of the old mill. Apparently the tree was planted by one of the quarry's managers many moons before the Sitka spruce invasion.

After the quarries had been passed we came to Pont Llaeron, which has often been described as a Roman bridge. Although the Romans would have marched through these parts – the foundations of one of their forts lie buried beneath a Cwrt farmhouse (Cefn-caer) in the Dyfi Valley – the present structure is a medieval packhorse bridge, also used later by cattle drovers.

Beyond the bridge a track led us to the col beneath Tarren y Gesail. Hereabouts the maps threatened us with many more trees than there were in real life; we climbed to the summit without hindrance along a pleasing edge overlooking a shadowy, rock-fringed cwm at the head of Nant Lliwdy.

The cloud had dispersed and shafts of sunlight played with the waters of the meandering Dyfi and its estuary. Our day, one of many on the Snowdonia to Gower long-distance route, ended with a dash down to Machynlleth in the fading evening light, but I've since been drawn back to the Tarrens many times.

Seen across the waters of the Dyfi estuary, the Tarrens present a splendid sight, with wooded foothills and twisting pastured vales leading the eye to steep-

Above: Nant Gwernol in the Tarren Hills near Abergynolwyn.

sided, sprawling ridges etched with faint craggy cwms. These mountains were populated in ancient times and there are many Bronze Age burial cairns on the western ridges. These ridges were also once tramped by pilgrims following St Cadfan's Way, a skyline route from Machynlleth to Tywyn. On reaching the coast, the ancient Christians would have continued their journey by sea to Bardsey Island.

Just beyond the Tarren hills are those of the Dyfi, with the little slate village of Corris lying in between. Here, you have three 2000-footers. The highest is Maesglase at 2218 feet/676 m, followed by Waun-oer and Cribin Fawr. Still troubled by the vast spruce plantations of the Dyfi Forest, these mountains are also known for their splendid grass ridges. To use a footballing analogy, the Dyfi Hills are in the same division as the Tarren but they might make the play-offs – the ridges are longer, the crags are more frequent and pronounced and there are some superb glacial cwms.

Above: The Tarren ridges are scattered with ancient cairns, this one on Trum Gelli.
Opposite: Maesglase and its waterfalls.

The best place for an exploration of the Dyfi Hills is Dinas Mawddwy, a beautifully sited village often also used as a base for the Aran mountains. Everything around Dinas is splendidly verdant, with the Dyfi and the Cerist rivers meandering through a patchwork of pastures and woodlands. The huge glacial cwm of Maesglase is one of the most spectacular sites in the region, with huge waterfalls tumbling down cliffs at its head.

Further up the road towards the Bwlch Oerddrws is Cwm Cerist, where the crags of Cribin Fawr and Craig Portas look down over a similar but slightly more austere hollow. The undulating ridges between these peaks are a joy to walk and offer wide views of the Snowdon mountains, the Mawddach and Dyfi estuaries, and the coast.

I've mentioned the spruce forests. Well, they're largely to the south and west of the main ridges and have spread deep into the cwms above Corris, Aberllefenni and Aberangell. Forestry tracks do, however, make possible fast inroads to the hills, especially so in Cwm Ratgoed.

Graig Goch and its neighbour Mynydd Rugog face the mighty Cadair Idris peaks across Tal-y-llyn and Lake Mwyngil and, although lower, put up a good fight for supremacy with their formidable crag-fringed escarpment plummeting in steep screes into the lake and surrounding pastures.

Dwarfed by these slopes is the little white-washed Ty'n y Cornel Inn, a place that has graced many Welsh postcards and calendars. The glacial U-shaped valley hereabouts is part of a massive geological tear fault running all the way from Tywyn on the coast to Bala. The south side of this valley has shifted around two miles north-eastwards compared to the north side. Before the rift, Graig Goch would probably have faced Foel Cae'rberllan, the peak above Abergynolwyn.

There are no direct routes up the north face of the mountain for the slopes are too steep and friable, and those to the south are cloaked in thick forestry with no rights of way leading to them. But all is not lost. An old miners' track beginning not far from the Ty'n y Cornel slants up the north slopes in magnificent fashion to meet the ridge at its north-eastern end. Just looking at the map tells you that Graig Goch will have magnificent views of Cadair Idris, and it does.

Opposite: Graig Goch and Tal-y-llyn with the Ty'n y Cornel Inn dwarfed by the mountain's slopes of crag and scree. Above: The top of Cadair Idris hides behind clouds in views across Tal-y-llyn from Graig Goch.

Route DT1
From Tal-y-llyn

A stimulating short walk with fine panoramas

Start: Roadside 200 yards/m east of Ty'n y
  Cornel Inn, Tal-y-llyn (GR: SH 715095)

Distance: 2½ miles/4km

Height gain: 1675ft/510m

Time: 1½ hours

Go through the gate at GR 715096 (just
north-east along the road from the Ty'n y Cornel Inn and at the edge of the access area)
and climb up the steep pathless slopes to an
old miners' path, which has strangely been
omitted from the latest OS maps. It rakes left
across the slopes of Graig Goch and Mynydd
Rugog, high above Llyn Mwyngil.

Where the fence alongside deviates left,
straddle it to continue by, and sometimes on
top of, a crumbling slate wall. The path veers
to the right across the north-east slopes of
Mynydd Rugog with views of Corris Uchaf
opening up. On reaching a cross-fence climb
to the right on the steep grass slopes of the
hill end to reach the rock-studded crest of
Mynydd Rugog. Join the vehicle track coming
in from the left and follow it to its terminus
just short of Graig Goch's rough, mossy top.
Go along the edges for the best views of
Cadair Idris and the lake.

*Note: Although forest tracks will lead across a
dip and up to Tarren y Gesail the plantations
are private with no rights-of-way.*

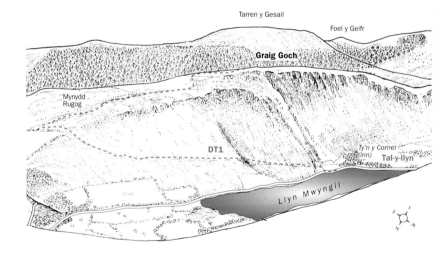

Opposite: On Mynydd Rugog with Cadair Idris ahead.

TARREN Y GESAIL

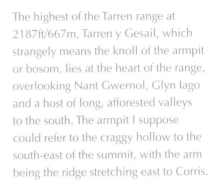

The highest of the Tarren range at 2187ft/667m, Tarren y Gesail, which strangely means the knoll of the armpit or bosom, lies at the heart of the range, overlooking Nant Gwernol, Glyn Iago and a host of long, afforested valleys to the south. The armpit I suppose could refer to the craggy hollow to the south-east of the summit, with the arm being the ridge stretching east to Corris.

The mountain is rather lacking in finesse – it's a bit of a hulk with steep grassy sides scarred with patches of friable crag rising to a square-cut crest. The craggy cwm to the south-east is disappearing slowly under creeping vegetation. Sadly, spruce trees are also spreading from the valley almost to the summit. Luckily its 2000ft altitude should save the mountain from being completely engulfed.

To the north-west Tarren y Gesail throws out a ridge to the outlier of Foel Pandy, a rough rocky knuckle with steep sides tumbling to the narrow ravine of Cwm Iago. This would be of great interest to the walker but for the fact that there is no access to the CROW land. Most ascents of Tarren y Gesail start from Abergynolwyn and take in the valley of Nant Gwernol, a fascinating place of quarrying relics and ancient highways. At

Left: The conifer-cloaked Tarren y Gesail seen at the end of Cwm Iago.

the southern foot of the mountain is Pont Llaeron, a well-preserved medieval packhorse bridge with lively cataracts flowing beneath its single arch.

Below: Crossing Pont Llaeron in Nant Gwernol.

Route DT2
Bryn Eglwys and Pont Llaeron
A fascinating route through history
Start: Abergynolwyn car park
   (GR: SH 677069)
Distance: 4 miles/6km
Height gain: 2055ft/630m
Time: 2½ hours

Follow the lane from Pandy Square opposite the Railway pub, climbing left past the café and up into Nant Gwernol. Down below you on the right is the bounding stream surrounded by beautiful deciduous woodland, which tempers the sight of conifers on the hills beyond. Ignore signs for the railway station: you're on the track up the valley.

The tarmac ends and there are two tracks ahead. The unwanted left fork zigzags up to Hendrewallog. Your track is the right fork, which continues up the valley with the first

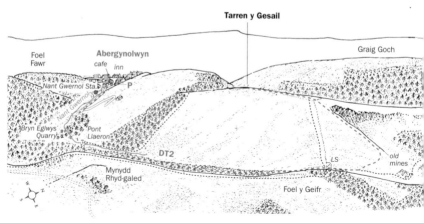

Above: Climbing above the crags of Tarren y Gesail's south-east ridge.

spoil heaps of Bryn Eglwys down in the bottom of the valley to your right. The crags of the rounded hill, Tarrenhendre, add considerable interest to the scene on the far side, although they are only just above the top edge of the spruce plantations.

Many relics of the bygone quarrying industry are seen hereabouts, in an area devastated by spoil heaps and mine shafts. The winding track passes a huge quarry pit, part hidden by trees. At one time this was bare and you could see two large but artificial waterfalls plummeting into its depths and a large incline climbing to a top pulley house. These days this fascinating scene has been obscured by thick woodland.

Beyond the pit the track swings right towards the main quarry. Part of the way around the bend, turn left on a signed path through conifers. This soon arcs right and continues up the valley on what can be a marshy grass path above the tree line. Where the main path turns left leave it for a path descending to an ancient one-arched stone bridge, Pont Llaeron, said to be of Roman origin but much more likely to be a medieval packhorse bridge.

Beyond the bridge, our path climbs the far bank before veering left at the edge of the plantations engulfing the slopes of Foel y Geifr. The path soon enters the woods and climbs parallel to the Nant Llaeron stream before emerging on the pass between Tarren y Gesail and Foel y Geifr.

You could turn left and climb the steep grass slopes by the fence to reach Tarren y Gesail's summit; but it's far better to go over the stile in the fence and keep straight ahead towards the quarry buildings at the head of the heavily afforested valley of Nant Lliwdy. Now aim for the south-east spur of the mountain for a climb alongside its eastern crags – pre-2007 OS maps show conifers here, but they don't exist today. Again it's steep but the views are wide and you're seeing Gesail's best side. After the pull to the ridge, it's just an easy promenade westwards on moor grass to the summit trig point.

Descent

Just head east until you come to the crag edge and follow it down towards the old mine levels at its foot. Turn right (south of west) around the slope, to reach the stile at the pass between Tarren y Gesail and Foel y Geifr.

Note: in poor conditions such as snow, ice or mist it might be prudent to descend south-east from the fence corner at the east end of the summit plateau at GR 714059 to reach the pass.

Turn right over the stile and follow the path down Nant Llaeron, through the conifers. Watch out for the little path on the right down to Pont Llaeron. Once over the bridge climb the far banks to a grass path heading down Nant Gwernol, with trees to the left. After entering the trees the path comes to a quarry track at Bryn Eglwys. Turn right along this. It will lead you to the lane heading back down the valley to Abergynolwyn.

Route DT3
Dyfi Bridge and Pantyspydded

A long forest route that has seen better days

Start: Dyfi Bridge, Machynlleth (GR: SH 744019), parking at roadside towards Machynlleth

Distance: 4 miles/6 km

Height gain: 2200ft/660m

Time: 2½ hours

Note: Forestry operations of the early 2000s have spoiled what used to be a wonderful route

---

From the bridge follow the A493 Aberdyfi road, then take the first turn right uphill on a narrow lane, which winds through pasture and woodland. Take the left fork beyond the cottage of Cwm gila. The views become increasingly good as the green lane climbs towards the vast plantations of the Dyfi Forest. Looking south you can see the rolling hills rising to Pumlumon; looking east more of the same.

The lane enters the forest and soon comes to a five-way junction (GR 730033). The track you want here is the third exit on the left. After heading WNW for a short way the path turns north. Ignore all turn-offs to reach a wide track to Pantyspydded (GR 729041), where a ruinous farmhouse has been converted for use as a shed.

Yellow markers to the left of the buildings guide the route up the afforested spur ahead,

Tarren y Gesail

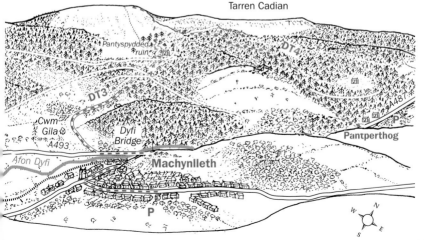

where little paths make short cuts across a zigzagging forestry track before emerging at a stile on the edge of a grassy hillside beneath the upper slopes of Tarren y Gesail (GR 720055). To the right are some old mine levels at the head of the valley of Nant Lliwdy. *Note: pre-2007 maps show trees here but they don't exist on the ground.*

Now head for the foot of Tarren y Gesail's slopes and climb on steep grassy slopes with the mountain's eastern crags on your right. After the stiff climb, head west along the grassy summit ridge to reach the trig point.

Descent

From the summit trig point head east along the crest until you come to the crag edge. Here you descend south-east on a grassy spur to its foot, with quarry workings to your left and ahead. Take care in wintry conditions, or else follow the fence-side path to the west.

The thickly afforested chasm of Nant Lliwdy stretches out ahead of you but ignore old mine paths descending into it. Instead take the thin path half-right (south-east). This leads to a stile into the forest at GR 720055.

Yellow markers help to locate the line of the old path, which diverts from the old forestry track in several places. After reaching the ruins of Pantyspydded (GR 728041) another waymark highlights the route to the right, which descends southwards on a less prominent forestry track. There are many new bulldozed tracks to the left and right hereabouts but ignore them.

At GR 730033 there is a meeting of five forestry tracks. Your route takes the continuing track in roughly the same direction as you've been going but it is offset slightly to the left. It heads south-eastwards to the plantation's edge. The green road that follows is a joy to descend, with airy views of the hills of Maesglase, Mynydd y Cemais and Pumlumon (Plynlimon) beyond the brilliant green fields of the Dyfi Valley. The track, tree-lined in the lower stages, meets a narrow tarmac lane by a house, Cwm gila (GR 736023), and this leads to the A493, just west of the Dyfi Bridge.

Right: On a cold Tarren y Gesail summit.
Opposite: The track from Pantperthog with the crags of Tarren y Gesail ahead.

Route DT4

Pantperthog

A straightforward, speedy and much prettier route than you'd expect

Start: Pantperthog, lay-by parking (GR: SH 750043

Distance: 3¼ miles/5.2 km

Height gain: 2130ft/650m

Time: 1½–2 hours

The grass bridleway marked on the map starts just to the left of Pantperthog's chapel and squeezes between it and a large house to enter the valley of Nant Siambr Wmffre (the last two words are pronounced something like 'shambar umphray'). Soon it joins a forestry road from the left and continues up the pleasantly wooded valley with the stream flowing in lively cataracts on the left. The conifers you might have expected are higher up the slopes and don't impose upon the scene.

Soon Tarren y Gesail's craggy south-east face appears above the trees. In the valley's upper regions, the conifers surround you but the firm track offers a quick way through them and the craggy spur to the left looks promising.

The track arcs left as it reaches the head of the valley under the crags of Tarren Cadian and further on it doubles back left and ceases to be of use. A short grass path at the apex of

the bend leads to the edge of the forest, where a stile allows access to the open hillside.

Tarren y Gesail now begins to dominate all, with the remains of old mining levels beneath it. A narrow grass path heads for the mines and bends left by some old shafts. The path should be abandoned on reaching the higher levels where you should turn right across tufty grass slopes to reach the foot of Tarren y Gesail's south-east spur.

Now the real climb begins. It's a tough but airy climb on grassy slopes above the rim of those crags. The toils end suddenly as you reach the eastern end of the summit crest. It's now a simple stroll on grass to reach the trig point.

Descent

From the trig point head east until you come to the crag edge and descend along it to its foot, where you'll see the ruins of the old mines below you and on the left. Now turn right (SSW) across rough grassy moorland to reach the stile at the pass between Tarren y Gesail and Foel y Geifr. Take care in wintry conditions, or else follow the fence-side path to the west (see Route DT2).

At the foot of the crags maintain direction towards the forestry plantations, but turn left on reaching a prominent narrow path which passes the old mine level before heading towards the forestry at the head of Nant y Darren. Go over the stile and take the short grass path to a hairpin bend in a forestry road. Take the lower course on the right. This curves right and descends the valley. Take the main right fork beyond a turning circle at GR 737054 and again the right fork at a sharp U-turn by another turning circle. This brings the route out to Pantperthog.

Other route options

It's perfectly feasible to follow Route DT2 to Pont Llaeron, but instead of descending to the bridge, keep to the main grass path entering the upper cwm on the north side of the stream. Where the forest on the left ends you can climb the extremely steep grass slopes at the forest's edge to the summit crest. This also makes a good quick route down.

Left: Above the mines at the head of Cwm Lliwdy.

RIDGE ROUTES

Tarrenhendre

Distance: 3 miles/5km
Height gain: 985ft/ 300m
Time: 1 ¼ hours

Head east across the crest until you reach a fence corner. Turn right here and descend the southern slopes to a pass where four paths meet (GR 717054). Go straight ahead into the forest, ignoring the path on the right, which goes down to Pont Llaeron. The path soon veers right and partly emerges from the forest, with trees now only on the right.

Continue along the crest, ignoring paths and tracks on the left. The rise to Tarrenhendre is steady, with a fence to guide you all the way. In the upper region the path gets quite close to the vegetated eastern crags. There's a low fence to cross before reaching the summit cairn.

Mynydd Rhyd-galed

Distance: 2 miles/3.3km
Height gain: 245ft/75m
Time: 1 ½ hours

As with the Tarrenhendre ridge route, head east across the crest until you reach a fence corner. Turn right here and descend the southern slopes to a pass where four paths meet (GR 717054). Go straight ahead into the forest, ignoring the path on the right, which goes down to Pont Llaeron. The path soon veers right and partly emerges from the forest, with trees now only on the right.

The shaley-cragged Mynydd Rhyd-galed is offset on the left from the ridge you're on, and once you've gone over Foel y Geifr you'll see a track to the left, which avoids the ascent of a subsidiary peak. Once you reach the grassy saddle connecting Mynydd Rhyd-galed with the main ridge turn left off the path, cross the fence on your left and make the short climb south-east to the summit.

MYNYDD RHYD-GALED

Mynydd Rhyd-galed, which means mountain of the harsh or dry ford, is a rounded peak surrounded by shaley crags. It's slightly offset from the main Tarren ridge and separates the valleys of Cwm Dwr and Cwm Breichiau.

As with most of the Tarrens, approaches from all sides are dominated by the spruce woods of the Dyfi Forest, although the rolling hillside to the south-west is prettily dressed with farm pastures and more natural woods.

Views to the north are blocked by the bulk of Tarren y Gesail but views southwards across the sandbars of the Dyfi Estuary and the softer hills of Mid Wales more than compensate. If it's clear enough you will be able to look over the shoulder of Pumlumon to the great sandstone escarpments of the Brecon Beacons.

Left: Mynydd Rhyd-galed from the slopes of Tarrenhendre.

Route DT5
Pennal and Mynydd Cefn-caer

*A pleasant route with wonderful
   retrospective views of the Dyfi Estuary*

Start: Pennal (GR: SH 699004) roadside
   parking

Distance: 2½ miles/4.1km

Height gain: 1605ft/490m

Time: 1½ hours

Follow the minor lane heading north through the village of Pennal before taking the left fork lane by a woodland copse. This passes through pastures with the meandering Afon Pennal to the left. The lane eventually descends to cross the river and continues towards Pennal Isaf.

At the end of the public road a waymarked path on the left takes the route above Esgair Isaf farm, before joining a track coming in from the farmhouse. This heads towards a forestry plantation at Esgair Uchaf but, just short of the trees, turn right to climb the pathless grassy spur. A track does develop further uphill as the forest's edge nears again, and takes the route across more pastures; but not far beyond a cross-wall it fades again.

Once over the next crest, Mynydd Cefn-caer, follow a line along the west side of the ridge and you'll pick up a faint track, which leads to another one emerging from the forestry plantations on your right. Go straight across this and climb the now-rougher moor grass hill to Mynydd Rhyd-galed's summit.

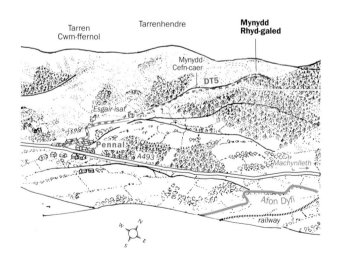

Opposite: Looking back to Pennal and the Dyfi Estuary from the track up Mynydd Cefn-caer.

Route DT6

Abergynolwyn and Bryn Eglwys

*A fine riverside stroll followed by rough
    forest rides to the ridge*

Start: Abergynolwyn (GR: SH 677069)

Distance: 2¾ miles/4.4km

Height gain: 1510ft/460m

Time: 1½ hours

A tarred lane climbs steeply from Pandy Square, past slate-built terraces and into woodland beyond, to emerge high on pastureland overlooking the trees of Nant Gwernol. The lane continues up the wooded ravine and passes beneath the ruins of Hendrewallog.

Take the less prominent right fork track up the valley (the left zigzags up to large barns on the hillside above you). Stay with this old quarry road as it passes the deep tree-enshrouded pits of the Bryn Eglwys quarry. On reaching some huge slag heaps leave the main track for a very faint path, which has been partially obscured by tree felling. This rounds the east and south sides of spoil heaps to reach a gap in a stone wall (GR 693051).

A yellow marker post on the left highlights the way up a forest ride. Follow this all the way to the stile on the plantation's upper edge just below the Tarren ridge a short distance west of Foel y Geifr.

After climbing to the ridge crest take the path that veers right (SSW) to round the next ridge-top summit. Mynydd Rhyd-galed is the craggy rounded peak offset from the main ridge but now straight ahead. The path soon reaches the grassy connecting saddle. Once on this leave the main path and climb south-east to Mynydd Rhyd-galed.

Other route options

There are numerous options using various forestry roads, but nothing very exciting.

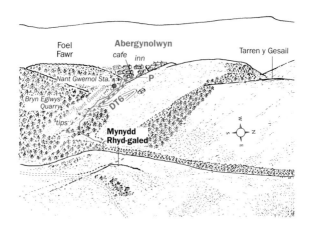

Above: Nant Gwernol and Abergynolwyn.

RIDGE ROUTES

Tarren y Gesail
Distance: 2 miles/3.3km
Height gain: 885ft/270m
Time: 1½ hours

Head north-west along the ridge to cross the stile in the fence. Beyond this turn right to follow a path that rounds the unnamed peak west of Foel y Geifr before joining the main ridge. Stay with the ridge fence and the crest over Foel y Geifr.

Although it's confined to the north side at first, the forest soon overwhelms the ridge and the path makes its way through the trees. It eventually bends left and descends to a stile at the edge of the forest (GR 717054). You can either climb the steep grass slopes ahead, following a fence to Tarren y Gesail's summit crest, where you turn left for the trig point, or turn right on a path heading towards the quarry and the foot of Gesail's craggy south-east spur.

Note: the trees shown hereabouts on pre-2007 OS maps do not exist on the ground.

Once at the foot of the spur climb north-west alongside the rim of the crags. This will take you to the east side of the summit crest, where there is a simple walk on a grass ridge to reach the trig point.

Tarrenhendre
Distance: 1½ miles/2.4km
Height gain: 790ft/240m
Time: 1 hour

Head north-west along the ridge but after about a hundred paces, descend left on to a wide vehicle track curving left on to the main Tarren ridge. Now climb by the fence on to Tarrenhendre's summit, which lies beyond a low cross-fence.

Tarrenhendre, the knoll of the winter dwelling, looks across the ravine of Nant Gwernol to Tarren y Gesail. It's a distinctively rounded peak with two sparse-cragged corries on its high eastern flanks and one on its grassy southern slopes above Pennal.

It is part of a complex series of ridges, but unlike the larger Tarren y Gesail, Tarrenhendre is integral to them all. One ridge radiates north-east over Foel y Geifr and terminates at the deep afforested Nant Lliwdy, while the south-west ridge stretches out nearly 7 miles/11km towards the sands of Tywyn on Cardigan Bay. The deep and attractive Dolgoch valley, where you'll see the famous Dolgoch Falls, bites deep into Tarrenhendre's western slopes.

Tarrenhendre is largely afforested on the north-eastern Nant Gwernol side, but to the south and west its slopes are free, with its ridges of grass and a little heather offering pleasant promenades with stunning views of the Dyfi Estuary and Cadair Idris. Here the Tarren Mountains are at their best.

Luckily for Tarren walkers, the Talyllyn Railway can be used to link ascents from Dolgoch, Rhyd-yr-onen and Abergynolwyn.

Opposite: Tarrenhendre seen from Bryn Eglwys.

Route DT7
Abergynolwyn and the north ridge
Route through deciduous and coniferous forest with a sting in the tail
Start: Abergynolwyn (GR: SH 677069)
Distance: 3 miles/5km
Height gain: 2065ft/630m
Time: 2 hours

Climb the lane from the back of Pandy Square but leave it for the path on the right, signed to Nant Gwernol station. The delightful path enters deciduous woodland and follows the north-east bank of the boisterous Nant Gwernol. After going to the right over a footbridge the path comes to the station, which is the terminus of the narrow-gauge Talyllyn Railway. Turn immediately left, then left again at a T-junction of paths.

This takes the route to the restored winding house at the top of the Allt Wyllt incline. Beyond this the route continues through the forest to reach the Nant Moelfre stream and the foot of the Cantybedd Incline. Do not cross the footbridge here but continue with the path to climb to a flinty forestry road, where you should turn left.

By now the deciduous trees have all but disappeared, replaced by ranks of spruce and larch, and the urge will be to stride quickly along the easy gradients of the roads. Take the right fork forestry road, then ignore the one doubling back right. The road then bends sharp left then sharp left again beneath the slopes of Foel Fawr – another right-turn road should be ignored between the two bends.

On reaching a forestry vehicle lay-by on the left look up to the hillside on the right towards a nick in the skyline. Your route to the top will climb to this. (Note: if you pass a wood cabin on the right-hand side of the forest road you've come about 50 yards/m too far.)

Recent tree-felling has made what used to be an obvious route up a forest ride a little more difficult, but a couple of slate scree patches just to the right of Tarrenhendre's crags show the rough direction. Higher up, the path enters a little gulley before reaching the ridge near some sheep pens. A steep climb left by the ridge fence leads to the summit.

Above: The climb up the steep little gorge to Tarrenhendre's north ridge.

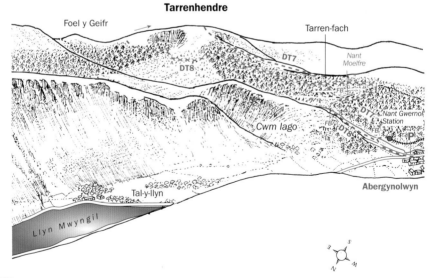

Tarrenhendre

Foel y Geifr

Tarren-fach

Nant Moelfre

DT7

DT8

Nant Gwernol Station

Cwm Iago

FB

DT18

Tal-y-llyn

Abergynolwyn

Llyn Mwyngil

Route DT8
Abergynolwyn and the east ridge

*A fine riverside stroll followed by rough
    forest rides to the ridge*

Start: Abergynolwyn (GR: SH 677069)
Distance: 4¼ miles/6.8km
Height gain: 2100ft/640m
Time: 2½ hours

From the car park in Pandy Square turn right along the lane as it climbs past the last of Abergynolwyn's terraces into the leafy environs of Nant Gwernol. As in DT7 leave it for the path on the right, signed to Nant Gwernol station. The well-graded path enters deciduous woodland and follows the north-east bank of the boisterous Nant Gwernol stream.

This time ignore the footbridge crossing to Nant Gwernol station, but continue on this side of the stream until you reach a second footbridge. Once over this turn left on a path that soon comes to the subsidiary stream Nant Moelfre, before climbing away to a forestry road. Turn left on the gently rising

flinty road, taking the right fork at the next junction, and then ignoring two more tracks on the right. Follow the road around two sharp left-hand bends.

Now you are high on the hillside with the slopes of Tarren-fach rearing up to the right and the quarries of Bryn Eglwys far below. The road passes an Outward Bound log cabin and winds around the high slopes of Tarrenhendre before ending at a turning circle (GR 688041). A green ride soon deteriorates into a very soggy path (marked with thin black dashes on OS Explorer maps). After crossing a small stream the now muddy path veers left and traces the upper edge of the trees before emerging beneath low vegetated cliffs high on Tarrenhendre's east ridge.

Ahead (to the east) you should see a line of old fence-posts. Head for these across slopes of heather, thick moss and bilberry. Now climb the easier ground alongside the posts to the ridge-fence, where you join the main Pilgrims' Way path, which climbs right to reach Tarrenhendre's summit.

Below: Tarrenhendre and the head of Nant Gwernol with the sun setting over the Dyfi Estuary.

Above: On Tarrenhendre's east ridge with Foel y Geifr ahead and Tarren y Gesail top right.

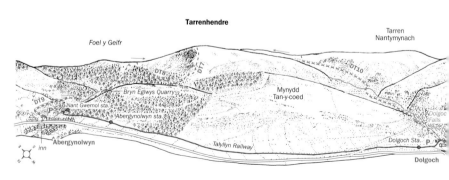

Route DT9
Abergynolwyn and Bryn Eglwys
Explores the old quarries of Nant Gwernol
Start: Abergynolwyn (GR: SH 677069)
Distance: 4 miles/6km
Height gain: 2035ft/620m
Time: 2½ hours

A tarred lane climbs steeply from Pandy Square, past slate-built terraces and into woodland beyond, to emerge high on pasture overlooking the trees of Nant Gwernol. Resist the temptation to follow waymarked paths on the right but stay with the lane as it passes beneath the ruins of Hendrewallog.

Take the less prominent right fork track up the valley (the left zigzags up to some large barns on the hillside above you). Stay with this old quarry road as it passes the deep tree-enshrouded pits of the Bryn Eglwys quarry. On reaching some huge slag heaps leave the main track for a very faint path, which has been partially obscured by tree felling. This rounds the east and south sides of slag heaps to reach a gap in a stone wall at GR 693051.

Ignore the yellow-tipped marker post by a narrow forest ride and instead keep to the edge of the plantation close to a stream on the right. After a short way the route climbs away from the stream through another forest ride on the left. Marshy in places, the ride leads the route to a wide opening at the top of the forest before climbing further to the col at Pant Gwyn, a spot marked by a ladder stile. Turn right and climb the steep grass slopes to Tarrenhendre.

Route DT10
The Dolgoch Falls
A spectacular wooded gorge with waterfalls followed by a wild cwm to the ridge
Start: Dolgoch Falls Hotel and café car park (voluntary donations collection box for upkeep of paths) (GR: SH 650046)
Distance: 3½ miles/5.5km
Height gain: 2035ft/620m
Time: 2½ hours

Follow the tourist route along a lane on the right side of the hotel. This passes the approach to Dolgoch station (on the Talyllyn narrow-gauge railway) and goes under the railway bridge. As the path enters the wooded ravine stay on the north-east bank of Nant Dolgoch to pass the thundering white waters of the lower, middle and upper falls.

On reaching (but not crossing) the footbridge at the head of the wooded ravine, climb left to a step stile leading to open hillsides, where the crusty crags and sparse scrub woods of Pen Trum-gwr are particularly impressive.

Double back left on a grassy track climbing to the stony right-of-way track heading up the valley. Soon you reach the confluence of the Sychnant and Dolgoch streams; the former cuts a deep hollow beneath Tarrenhendre and Mynydd Tan-y-coed, while the latter sneaks behind Tarrenhendre's west ridge.

Take the right fork track by the confluence to ford Nant Sychnant. This follows Nant Dolgoch's east bank to some sheepfolds before crossing the stream and climbing beneath the

crags of Tarren Nantymynach. Leave the track for the second of two side tracks on the right, which climbs towards the ridge at Mynydd Esgairweddan.

A short trek leads to the ridge-top where views of the Dyfi Estuary open up. Climb left by the fence to the cairn at a fence intersection near the top. Turn left for the summit of Tarrenhendre.

Note: Those who do not want to visit the more formal paths surrounding the Dolgoch Falls can take the old track climbing south from Ty-gwyn (north of the Dolgoch station and hotel), over the Talyllyn Railway at the Quarry Siding Halt. This wilder route traverses hillsides above the valley bottom and is joined by the main route above the Dolgoch woods.

Opposite: The Dolgoch Falls.
Below: The rugged Nant Dolgoch valley above the falls.

Route DT11

Pennal and Mynydd Cefn-caer

A pleasing route with great southern
*   panoramas*

Start: Pennal (GR: SH 700004)

Distance: 4 miles/6km

Height gain: 2000ft/610m

Time: 2½ hours

Follow the minor lane through the village before taking the left fork towards Pennal Isaf. A waymarked path on the left takes the route above Esgair Isaf farm before joining a track coming in from the right. This heads towards a forestry plantation.

Just short of the trees turn right to climb the grassy spur of Mynydd Cefn-caer (a ladder stile in a cross-wall aids route-finding). The route is joined from the right by a slate track that rounds the west side of Mynydd Rhyd-galed to join the main Tarren ridge. Turn left up the fenced ridge to Tarrenhendre.

Other route options

There is no end to the combination of forestry routes to Tarrenhendre, from both Abergynol-wyn and Pennal, but most are rather dull. A reasonable option is to follow Route DT6 from Pennal then turn off to the farm of Rhos-farch (GR 695013), where a zigzag track climbs a pastured spur on to the open hillside of Tarren Rhosfarch. From the top of the ridge it's a short walk northwards to Tarrenhendre.

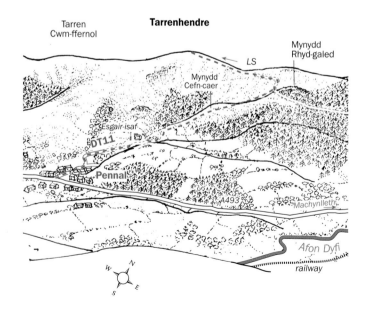

RIDGE ROUTES

Tarren y Gesail

Distance: 3 miles/5km
Height gain: 1050ft/ 320m
Time: 2 hours

From the summit head south-east, cross the stile in the fence at the south end of the summit, then follow the fence down the east ridge (the fence should be on your left). Stay with the ridge, ignoring a prominent track on the right which skirts Mynydd Rhyd-galed, and after a short descent, climb over Foel y Geifr. Beyond this the path enters the forest, which now engulfs the ridge, before descending again to a stile in a fence at the edge of the woods (GR 717054).

From here you can either climb the steep grass slopes ahead, following a fence to Tarren y Gesail's summit crest, where you turn left for the trig point, or turn right on a path heading towards the quarry and the foot of Gesail's craggy south-east spur.
Note: the trees shown hereabouts on the pre-2007 OS maps do not exist on the ground.

Once at the foot of the spur climb north-west alongside the rim of the crags. This will take you to the east side of the summit crest, where there is a simple walk on a grass ridge to reach the trig point.

Mynydd Rhyd-galed

Distance: 1½ miles/2.4km
Height gain: 245ft/75m
Time: 1 hour

From the summit head south-east, cross the stile in the fence at the south end of the summit, then follow the fence down the east ridge (the fence should be on your left). On the approach to an unnamed subsidiary summit, take the prominent track on the right. This arcs around right towards the crags of Mynydd Rhyd-galed. Just beyond a ladder stile at GR 700042, climb left by the fence on to a grassy saddle connecting the mountain with the Foel y Geifr ridge. Now turn right for the last easy climb to Mynydd Rhyd-galed's summit.

Trum Gelli

Distance: 2¼ miles/4.4km
Height gain: 295ft/95m
Time: 1½ hours

From the summit head south, following the ridge fence around the head of Nant Dolgoch to Tarren Rhosfarch. The snaking grass and heather ridge now heads south-west before climbing west on to the east summit of Tarren Cwm-ffernol. The higher east summit has a cairn with plaques commemorating mountain rangers.

Ahead now you'll see the larger cairns on Trum Gelli, and it's a straightforward walk by the fence south-westwards, then south to get to them.

Above: Trum Gelli from Tarren Cwm-ffernol.

Trum Gelli, the ridge of the grove,
lies halfway along the ridge stretching
south-west from Tarrenhendre and
declining gradually to the seaside
at Tywyn. It overlooks the conifers
of Cwm Ffernol to the south, but
otherwise this fine peak is wild and
untroubled by modern man.

This was not always so, for the hills around
here were populated by Iron and Bronze Age
peoples. Trum Gelli has two cairns, one
pyramidal and the other in a beehive shape.

Although largely grassy, the mountain
does have its share of crags, some above
the conifers of Cwm Ffernol and with rocky
outcrops spread across its sprawling west
face. A wonderful old highway straddles
these western slopes on its way from Pennal
to the Dysynni Valley. Unfortunately on some
weekends you'll see groups of four-wheel-
drive vehicles taking advantage of this road,
churning their way across the mountains.

Route DT12
Bryncrug and Nant Braich-y-rhiw

A beautiful valley approach

Start: Bryncrug (GR: SH 609033), parking in
    the village

Distance: 4 miles/6.6km

Height gain: 1800ft/550m

Time: 2½ hours

Head south through the village then along
the B4405 (in the Abergynolwyn direction) to
the bend at GR 611028, Pen-y-parc. Turn
right here along the winding country lane to
pass a campsite and Rhyd-yr-onen station on
the Talyllyn narrow-gauge railway.

Now the lane enters the splendidly attractive valley of Nant Braich-y-rhiw. The trees
surrounding the stream thin out to reveal lush
pastures as the tarmac ends. A lovely grassy
track continues with the gorse-lined stream
on the right through folds of hills, which
always reminds me of the College Valley in
the Cheviots of Northumberland.

The hillsides become wilder and the track,
now more stony, reaches a high pass marked
by a wooden footpath signpost. A smaller
wooden post on the left marks the start of the
path to the hills – the green swathe of the path
is visible on the hillside beyond. After an
uncertain start, the path forges its way up
grassy slopes and rakes along Trum Gelli's
south-western flanks. The wide southern
views now include the meandering Afon Dyfi
and its estuary and the Pumlumon Hills.

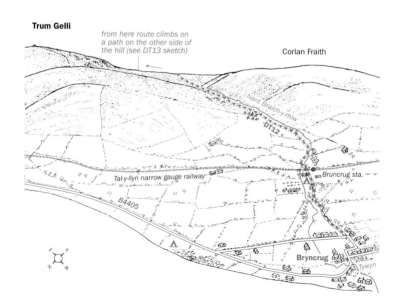

Trum Gelli

from here route climbs on
a path on the other side of
the hill (see DT13 sketch)

Corlan Fraith

Nant Braich-y-rhiw

DT12

Tal-y-llyn narrow gauge railway

Bruncrug sta.

B4405

Bryncrug

Tywyn

Above: Descending the track down Nant Braich-y-rhiw towards Bryncrug.

Route DT13
Cwrt and Allt Gwyddgwion
Following high ridges in the footsteps of the pilgrims

Start: Cwrt (GR: SH 688002)
Distance: 4 miles/6.5km
Height gain: 1770ft/540m
Time: 2½ hours

From the car park at Cwrt follow the minor lane climbing westwards. To your right you'll soon see the Afon Cwrt, a beautiful, swift-flowing stream tumbling on its stony bed through the shadows of its woodland setting. At a sharp left-hand bend near the farm at Pant-yr-on you'll see a right-forking stony track taking the route west, weaving through craggy knolls to a gate at GR 647001.

Here look northwards to the slopes of Allt Gwyddgwion to locate a green track that ascends to the huge cairn on Trum Gelli (not the lower track, which is more prominent early on). Follow this as it rakes across the slopes of Allt Gwyddgwion. It eventually reaches the ridge just short of the southern cairn on Trum Gelli.

Other route options
It would be possible to start at Dolgoch, taking the track to the head of the cwm at Mynydd Esgairweddan then following the ridge over Tarren Cwm-ffernol to the summit cairn. That is Route DT10 to the ridge, then the ridge route from Tarrenhendre to Trum Gelli.

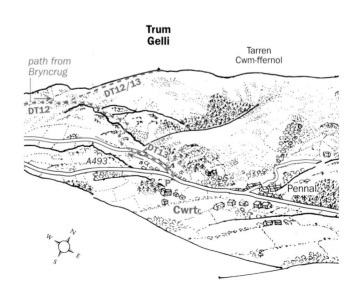

RIDGE ROUTE

Tarrenhendre

Distance: 2¾ miles/4.4km
Height gain: 640ft/195m
Time: 1¾ hours

From the highest summit cairn, follow the ridge fence north then north-east to round the conifers of Cwm Ffernol. Soon you reach the cairned summit of Tarren Cwm-ffernol, where the ridge turns west. Below you to the left is the bare valley of Nant Dolgoch, and the grass and heather ridge and its fence gradually arc around the head of this to reach the rounded summit of Tarrenhendre.

Below: The track to Trum Gelli from near Cwrt with the Dyfi Valley and the foothills of Pumlumon below.

Opposite: Llyn Foel Dinas from Route DT14.

Foel Dinas, the bare hill of the fort, is a steep-sided hill overlooking Dinas Mawddwy and the Afon Dyfi. It's mushroom-shaped in plan and has a lake sheltering in a shallow hollow set high up in desolate, windswept moorland to the east of the summit. The many-humped summit, which has a covering of bilberry and a little heather, has no cairn but its views of Cwm Maesglase are outstanding, with the cliffs and waterfalls of the valley being just a stone's throw away.

The east side of the hill is given up entirely to conifers, as is its western 'armpit' from the pass Bwlch Siglen to Blaen y Cwm. At Bwlch Siglen and on the northern slopes the heather and bilberry recede and give way to gorse and thick bracken, which can clog up the paths in parts during the summer months.

Minllyn, one of the more fascinating places on the hill, lies halfway up the slopes above Dinas Mawddwy's Buckley Pines Hotel. It started as an open hillside quarry but later mines were excavated. It produced slabbed slate, reduced in a processing mill on the higher level. Tramways descended to an exit incline which descended further into the valley and the old railway at Dinas Mawddwy. This in turn led to the Cambrian Coast Railway near Cemaes Road. The mines closed in 1925.

Route DT14
Dinas Mawddwy and the Minllyn Mine
A pleasant route with spectacular mining chasms and great ridge-top views

Start: Dinas Mawddwy lay-by on A470 just south of the village (GR: SH 859141)
Distance: 1¾ miles/2.8km
Height gain: 1245ft/380m
Time: 1–1½ hours

From the lay-by head north towards the village, but watch out for a forest path on the left-hand side of the road. Even the signpost hides behind foliage. The path angles up the afforested hillslopes and crosses a stony forestry road before coming to a ladder stile by some huge piles of slate – the edge of the deserted but spectacular Minllyn Slate Mine.

I was hoping to use the zigzag path climbing generally northwards towards Llyn Foeldinas but it has long ceased to be used and now lies choked and infested by rampant bracken. Instead I plumped for the path heading WSW from the mine to the south ridge of Foel Dinas.

To do this, from a stile in a wire fence follow waymarks ahead, to pass left in front of a long, ruined building, which was the mine's processing mill. An incline on the far side next to a tunnel entrance climbs to a huge pit with a waterfall flowing into it. The pit should be passed on the left. A steep climb brings the route to an even larger cavern with cliffs often frequented by climbers. Here the path veers left before climbing the narrow grassy hollow formed by a small stream. Climb through the pathless hollow, keeping left of the stream.

The route gets steep but manageable as it approaches the second of two prominent trees in the hollow. The map shows another tramway here, but in reality it is lost in the tufty grasslands. Sheep-tracks lead the route amiably along its former course to the ridge, where views of the afforested Cwm Glanmynach open up. Looking back you'll see magnificent landscapes where the velvety verdant lower Aran ridges are etched with hedgerow and woodland, while the craggy cone of Aran Fawddwy peeps out from their ridge-tops.

Climb northwards on the tufty grass of the ridge. Llyn Foeldinas appears, acting as a perfect foil for Aran Fawddwy, which has been rising into the skies with your every footstep along the ridge. Two fences meet to the east of the summit. Cross them at this intersection before turning left to the grassy unmarked summit, taking in those splendid views of Maesglase's crags and waterfalls along the way.

Other route options

It is possible to start from Aberangell and access the hill from Cwm Glanmynach and Blaen y Cwm before heading north across the grass slopes of Waun Fach. You could also divert from Maesglase's Route DT15 at Bwlch Siglen.

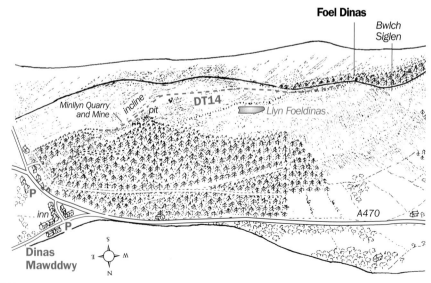

146

RIDGE ROUTE

Maesglase

Distance: 2¼ miles/3.6km
Height gain: 1245ft/380m
Time: 1½ hours

The route starts in fine fashion with a steep drop on a grassy spur towards Bwlch Siglen. However, beyond a ladder stile, the ground beneath your feet begins to get choked with low gorse, which hides among the bilberry, heather and bracken. As the path nears the bwlch it gets infested with bracken for a short way but things do improve as you climb out on a winding path up the spur ahead, which is cloaked with bilberry.

On reaching the rim of the moor, the best path to Maesglase sidles off right, eventually to cross the stream above Craig Maesglase's waterfalls, then follows the rim of the cliffs to the summit.

The 'real' but rather duller ridge route alternative ignores the right turn and instead continues uphill by the forest's edge to the ridge-top, before turning right alongside a fence climbing a broad grass and heather ridge towards Maesglase's summit. The fence veers right as it nears the highest top above Craig Rhiw-erch.

Below: The Minllyn Mine looking back to Coed Foeldinas.

Maesglase, which would be more correctly spelled Maesglasau – the blue or green meadows – is the highest of the Dyfi hills. The top known as Maen Du, the black stone, was once believed to be the highest (2210ft/674m), but a recent survey showed a western outlier Craig Rhiw-erch to be higher at 2218ft/676m.

The two summits overlook four beautiful glacier-carved corries: Cwm Cerist, an unnamed one beneath the rocks of Craig Rhiw-erch to the north-west, Cwm yr Eglwys and Cwm Maesglase. These corries are divided by exciting narrow grassy ridges and spurs, which plunge from summit to valley floor.

The greenness that gives the mountain its name can be seen to perfection as you walk though the pastures of Cwm Maesglase to its head. This is offset, but only gently, by the fringe of crags above you and the ravine, down which plunge the white waters of the falls. These falls have been known to ice up in winter to form an even greater spectacle.

Opposite: Maesglase's south ridge.

Route DT15
Cwm Maesglase and Bwlch Siglen
A classic route with a cliff-top finale

Start: Dinas Mawddwy – small lay-by on
   A470 1 mile/1.6km north of the village
   (GR: SH 848155)
Distance: 3½ miles/5.6km
Height gain: 2035ft/620m
Time: 2 hours

Follow the narrow tarred lane from the A470 past the cottages at Ffridd-gulcwm before taking a left fork track through a gate, just before the lane descends to turn right across the river. As you continue the walk there are increasingly wonderful views towards the end of the valley, where the slopes, cliffs and waterfalls of Maesglase rise from lush pastures.

The track tucks beneath the steep grass and bracken cloaked flanks of Foel Dinas and passes beneath some larch woods. Beyond a ladder stile beyond the woods, the track becomes rush-filled and walkers follow a little path to the left, before continuing past the relics of old quarries. A slaty path then climbs towards the pass of Bwlch Siglen. At the col the vast conifers of the Dyfi Forest are spread before your eyes. A few small pastures have stopped their spread in the cwm beyond.

From the col you need to climb up a spur of grass, bilberry and bracken, which lies to the left of a stream tumbling down the slopes.

In its upper reaches, the narrow path veers to the right across grassy moorland slopes with the cliffs out of view until there's a slight descent towards a huge domed crag at the top of the falls. The path crosses the stream above those falls – it's a spectacular sight to look down from the edge, but be careful.

The path continues in fine fashion above the cliffs before climbing to the first summit, where you look down into Cwm yr Eglwys (church corrie). Turn left for the brief climb to Maen Du, then onwards by the fence at first before veering right (west) to the small cairn on the main summit.

Above: Looking up Cwm Maesglase.

Route DT16
Coed Foeldinas and Bwlch Siglen

Offering splendid high-level views of Cwm Maesglase, after a dull start

Start: Lay-by at the north edge of Dinas Mawddwy village on the A470 (GR: SH 855149)

Distance: 4 miles/6.4km

Height gain: 2245ft/685m

Time: 2½ hours

A signposted footpath begins on some steps at the north end of the lay-by. It climbs the afforested lower slopes of Foel Dinas to a flinty forestry track. After turning right along the track for about 50 yards/m, another way-mark highlights a partially stepped path zig-zagging up through more conifers before angling right (west) high above the valley of the Cerist.

The path steepens and zigzags in more steps to reach a step stile leading out of the forest and on to the grassy northern slopes of

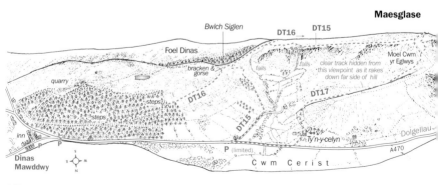

Foel Dinas. The path now traces the upper edge of the forest, now on your right, before traversing the open slopes high above Cwm Maesglase's verdant fields. At the end of the hollow are the cliffs of Maesglase and some waterfalls tumbling down from a nick in the cliffs.

In its later stages, the narrow path crosses a ladder stile over a fence and becomes choked with thickets of gorse, bracken, bilberry and heather, but things ease as you reach the pass of Bwlch Siglen. From here you climb steeply on the right-hand one of two paths, which winds up slopes of bilberry with a stream just to its right.

As it rounds the top of the stream, the path swings right and you could follow it as in Route DT15, but I'll offer an alternative, albeit a less spectacular way. This time stay by the forest's edge to reach an intersection of fences on a broad ridge. Turn right across heathery moorland to climb the ridge to the highest summit, Craig Rhiw-erch.

Route DT17
Ty'n-y-celyn and Moel Cwm yr Eglwys

A pleasing concessionary route on a fine farmers' track to the tops

Start: Dinas Mawddwy – small lay-by on A470 north of village (GR: SH 848155)

Distance: 3½ miles/5.6km

Height gain: 2035ft/620m

Time: 2½ hours

From the lay-by turn right up the road in the Dolgellau direction. After around 500 yards/m, cross the road and continue along the drive of Ty'n-y-celyn farm. This is a Tir Gofal concessionary route, so be considerate.

After turning left and passing in front of the farm turn right to go through the gate giving access to a waymarked track which climbs across pastures at first, then open hillside high above Cwm yr Eglwys (church valley). The fine grassy track, now lined with rushes, rakes high across the side of Moel Cwm yr

Right: At Bwlch Siglen.

151

Eglwys but never quite reaches the summit (it's only a small detour to the right once you reach the ridge).

On reaching the ridge the real climbing starts. The zigzagging track shown on OS Explorer maps does exist but it is very faint in places. It does however keep the gradients to a minimum. You can see the first part of it angling up right on the slopes ahead, passing patches of mining spoil.

Round the corner it will wind up a grassy spur before fading on the high slopes, where it's just a case of continuing up the spur to a step stile in the ridge fence just east of the Maen Du summit. Now it's an easy stroll by the fence at first, then west across heather to the little cairn on the main west summit overlooking the rocks of Craig Rhiw-erch.

Tougher walkers will shun the zigzag route for a little path following a fence up a tremendously steep grassy spur. Thankfully the toils are soon over and you find yourself standing on the summit of Maen Du. Again you would turn right to reach Craig Rhiw-erch.

Other route options

You could follow forestry tracks up the valley of the Afon Angell west of Aberangell village and climb on to the hill from the quarry track at GR 818124. It all looks a bit dull as a route. Routes from the east side of Cwm Cerist are possible but arduous when you tackle the slopes direct, as are the bracken-infested slopes beneath Craig Buarth-glas just off the A470.

RIDGE ROUTES

Foel Dinas

Distance: 2¼ miles/3.6km
Height gain: 625ft/190m
Time: 1¼ hours

___

From the west summit make your way east to the ridge fence, which leads to Maen Du. Now descend south-east above rocks to an outlying summit, which sends a spectacular narrow grassy spur into Cwm Maesglase (don't go down this). Continue southwards on a narrow path with cliffs to your left before crossing a stream above some fine waterfalls.

The path climbs out of the stream valley before traversing grassy moorland with a spruce plantation now lying ahead. Soon the path veers left down a grass and bracken spur, winding down to the right of a tumbling stream over patches of bilberry, parallel to, but some way from, the forest's northern edge.

Beyond the pass of Bwlch Siglen the route climbs up a spur entangled with gorse and bracken where it's not advisable to wear shorts! Eventually free of the undergrowth, the path climbs to a stile then up to the summit of Foel Dinas.

Craig Portas

Distance: 1¼ miles/1.8km
Height gain: 310ft/95m
Time: 1 hour

___

From Maesglase's west summit return to the ridge fence near to the point where it angles southwards. Follow it in this direction, but at a fence intersection go right over a step stile and follow the new fence westwards. Soon the route descends on a narrowing ridge with the crags of Cribin Fawr and Craig Portas adding interest to the scene.

The deep glacial scoop of Cwm Cerist opens up to your right and forestry to your left. Beyond a small eastern summit the ridge narrows again and you trace the cliff-edge right to the summit of Craig Portas.

Opposite: On Maesglase, descending one of the splendid ridges of the Dyfi hills towards Moel Cwm yr Eglwys.

Craig Portas lies at the head of three valleys: the heavily afforested Cwm Ceiswyn, Cwm Angell, and the fine glaciated corrie of Cwm Cerist, where it faces the crags of Cribin Fawr. The summit also sends out three ridges: a long south-western one terminating at Mynydd Dolgoed, a short interconnecting ridge with Cribin Fawr, and a marvellously narrow, undulating ridge to Maesglase.

Like most of the Dyfi hills, Craig Portas has its shaley vegetated cliffs, which overlook Cwm Cerist. It has two summits, the east one with a spot height of 1926ft/587m and the higher west one above the cliffs – both of which tantalisingly just fail to reach the magic 2000ft mark.

Route DT18
Cwm Ratgoed and Mynydd Dolgoed
A walk with views of forestry and mining
Start: Aberllefenni (GR: SH 770099)
Distance: 4 miles/6.4km
Height gain: 1835ft/560m
Time: 2–2½ hours

Follow the lane through the village, taking the right turn at the next junction to pass the bus turnaround and the mountain centre. Just beyond the sharp left-hand bend into Cwm Ratgoed, leave the road for a stony track on its left, continuing through the forest and parallel to the road.

On reaching a clearing, take a right fork that crosses a bridge spanning the Nant Ceiswyn and continues up the valley, one side of which is afforested and the other with disused slate tips, mine levels and high pastures. You are now walking along the Ratgoed Tramway, which linked the quarry with the Corris Railway at Aberllefenni, thus providing transport for the slate. The quarry closed in 1946.

The old tramway leads through an area of oak woods. Relics of machinery and buildings are scattered beneath the trees, many completely hidden. The only quarry building still inhabited is Plas Ratgoed (Ratgoed Hall

Opposite: Craig Portas from Maesglase ridge.
Left: The old mine buildings in Cwm Ratgoed.

on maps), which was the quarry owner's house.

Once past this large, slate-built house, look to the right across the fields towards the ruins of a stone-built barn, the key to the indistinct route to the ridge. The map shows the right of way cutting back to the right from the next old farmhouse, Dolgoed, but there are no stiles in the edges of the hayfield to be crossed.

The way around this obstacle (and this was endorsed by the farmer) is to head up the preceding pasture directly towards the barn where there's an open gateway tangled with high vegetation in the adjacent wall. Turn right by the wall and go over a step stile in a cross-fence. A tree-lined, grooved, grassy channel of a path slants up the hillside, then continues as a faint gravelly path along loose slopes beneath scrubby woodland.

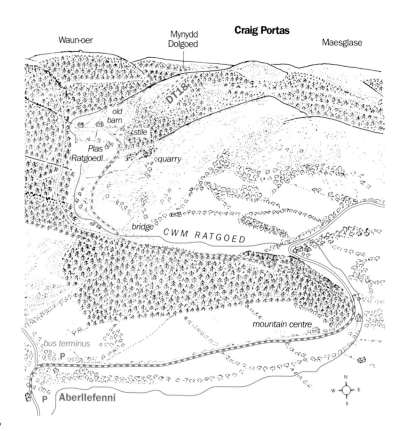

156

You will come to a fence, where there is a profusion of faint tracks used by previous walkers. You may notice slip marks, for the extremely steep hillside hereabouts consists of slate and clay – so take care. Climb alongside the fence but ignore the stile in it and continue to the top of the woods. Here the going gets easier on a high pastured ridge with coniferous forestry to the right.

As height is gained along the ridge the buttresses of Mynydd Moel, the second highest peak of the Cadair Idris range, comes into view. Gradually Penygadair and Gau Graig rise above the forests cloaking the west side of Cwm Ratgoed.

The ridge becomes quite knobbly and ill-defined as far as Mynydd Dolgoed. Now Craig Portas comes into view. From here it's a rounded grassy bump on the ridge, for the crags are on the north side. A steady climb leads to the grassy summit, where most walkers will detour to that attractive northern edge.

Below: The grassy Mynydd Dolgoed ridge to Craig Portas.

RIDGE ROUTES

Maesglase
Distance: 1¼ miles/1.8km
Height gain: 525ft/160m
Time: 1 hour

A fence will guide you nearly all the way to Maesglase's west summit. From Craig Portas descend along the top edge of the cliffs, then over the east summit before climbing the moor-like slopes to the south of Craig Rhiwerch. Turn left with the fence but where it turns right, go straight on to reach the little summit cairn.

Cribin Fawr
Distance: 1 mile/1.5km
Height gain: 345ft/105m
Time: ¾ hour

Again a fence guides you all the way between the summits. This time descend north with cliffs and the deep scoop of Cwm Cerist on your right. The descent is short and soon you're climbing up to Cribin Fawr. The wide ridge gets a bit marshy at times.

All the drama of Cribin Fawr lies to your right and when you reach its featureless summit, the urge will be to move on. If you want to see the best of the crags head eastwards to the cliff-edge above Cwm Cerist, then continue to the rocky bluff (near the 616m spot height) at its head.

Cribin Fawr lies on the north-west side of the Dyfi Hills. It's an austere hill sending out a crag-interspersed ridge declining to the wild pass of Bwlch Oerddrws in the north, and overlooking the upper cirque of Cwm Cerist to the east. Here the hillsides have been quarried and mined at Cloddfa Gwanas.

Cribin Fawr in a literal sense means the big skinflint, though most writers translate it as the big rocky crest (Crib Fawr). When you're walking on its featureless, slightly marshy, ridges you might be forgiven for thinking the former is correct. However, seen from Cwm Cerist below, Cribin Fawr has a fine rim of crags and splintered cliffs on its north and east sides, something you'd never know when standing at the summit fence intersection.

Usually Cribin Fawr is a step along the way to a long ridge walk, either to Waun-oer or Maesglase, but it would make sense to explore the summit area more fully and head east for those edges to take a look down the little ravine where the Afon Cerist is born.

Route DT19
Bwlch Oerddrws and Craig y Bwlch

A pleasing fairly easy route with fine views
Start: Bwlch Oerddrws (GR: SH 802170)
Distance: 1½ miles/2.3km
Height gain: 970ft/295m
Time: 1 hour

Go over the stile and follow the fence up towards the crags on a path that initially can be quite boggy. Things soon improve as the grass path winds between bluffs of Craig y Bwlch.

The path soon reaches and follows the ridge fence to reach the quarry of Cloddfa Gwanas, a fascinating place where the quarry tramway has been blasted out of the rocks of the ridge. There are two deep pits and an array of old buildings.

The head of Cwm Cerist on the left is fringed with the vegetated crags of Cribin Fawr and the steep grass slopes of Maesglase, while Cadair Idris and the Rhinog mountains dominate the western horizon. In between you should just be able to see the outlying houses of Dolgellau.

Stay with the fence to the left of the crest and alongside the rim of Cwm Cerist all the way to Cribin Fawr's unmarked grassy summit – following the rock crest to the right would, strangely, lead away from main ridge.

Opposite: Cribin Fawr seen across Bwlch Oerddrws.

Other route options

A recent Tir Gofal access agreement has made possible a route starting from Gwanas (GR 770168) just east of the Cross Foxes Inn. An access track heads south, keeping the two Gwanas farms to the left before turning left (the second track after Gwanas Fawr) to climb rough enclosures.

Take the left fork just south of the trees of Coed y Marthog and climb on rock-interspersed grass slopes before passing through a plantation of conifers. The track continues to climb to the Cloddfa Gwanas mines where you join the north ridge and Route DT19. Head south for the summit.

RIDGE ROUTES

Waun-oer

Distance: ¼ mile/1.2km
Height gain: 330ft/100m
Time: ½ hour

Keep the fence to the right by going over the two summit stiles at a fence intersection. The descent to the col soon steepens and forestry at the head of Cwm Ratgoed soon comes into view. The path is in places squeezed towards the fence by the trees. Heather now predominates on slaty slopes. A zigzag path climbs steeply up the other side, then the path levels out to reach the summit obelisk.

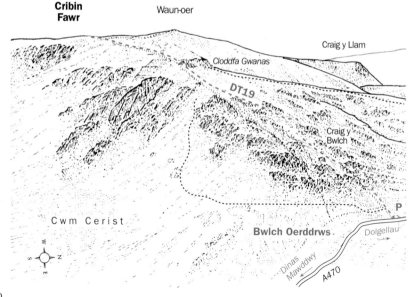

Craig Portas
Distance: 1 mile/1.5km
Height gain: 195ft/60m
Time: ¾ hour

Go over the stile by the fence intersection just south-west of the summit and head SSE along the south ridge at the head of Cwm Ratgoed's conifer-filled valley. The vegetated rock fringe of Craig Portas and the steep grassy slopes of Maesglase feature in the views ahead. From the col between Cwm Cerist and Cwm Ratgoed the ridge becomes steeper and narrower than it has been thus far, and the route climbs directly by the fence to the grassy summit.

Below: View from the slopes of Craig y Bwlch above Bwlch Oerddrws.

Above: The summit of Waun-oer.

Waun-oer, the cold moor, is the second-highest Dyfi peak: part of a long grassy ridge rising from the quarries of Aberllefenni to the pass of Bwlch Oerddrws. A grassy mountain scattered with crag, it has one north-eastern face of vegetated broken cliffs, which are steadily being engulfed by the dark blue-green foliage of the Sitka spruce. The trees cover the whole of the eastern Cwm Ratgoed side of the ridge.

The summit is topped by a fine cylindrical stone trig point, which offers some of the finest views of Cadair Idris, with the great mountain's crags paraded across the length of Cwm Rhwyddfor. A long grassy ridge continues south-west to the next peak, Mynydd Ceiswyn, then on to its end at Mynydd y Waun. To the west of the peak you'll see a long lane used by cyclists. This is Sarn Helen, the Roman road travelling the length of Wales.

Route DT20
Cwm Rhwddfor and Mynydd Ceiswyn
A steady plod followed by a fine ridge

Start: Roadside car park near the top of Cwm Rhwyddfor (GR: SH 753136)

Distance: 2¾ miles/4.3km

Height gain: 1490ft/455m

Time: 1½ hours

From the car park cross the road and go over the ladder stile, before turning left along rough grassland beneath the dark cliffs of Craig y Llam. At another roadside ladder stile (which you don't cross), climb half-right on a path climbing up a stony gully north of the cliffs. As the ground levels out the path becomes fainter and traverses wet, rushy ground. It crosses Sarn Helen, a Roman highway, now sadly tarred for the convenience of touring cyclists.

Now the path is only just discernable as it heads south-west across even wetter ground punctuated by several small streams, which hide in the rushes and sphagnum moss. The

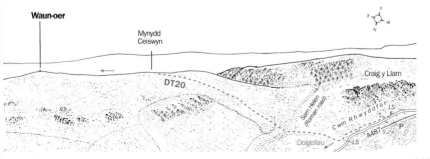

ground steepens again and sheep-tracks take you to the ridge, where you should arrive by a ladder stile. Turn left here and climb by the ridge fence over the subsidiary top of Mynydd Ceiswyn to the summit.

Below: Strolling over Mynydd Ceiswyn's ridge towards Waun-oer.

Route DT21
Aberllefenni and Cwm Ratgoed
An easy but dull forestry approach
Start: Aberllefenni (GR: SH 770099)
Distance: 4½ miles/7.3km
Height gain: 2065ft/630m
Time: 2–2½ hours

Follow the lane through the village before making a right turn at the next junction to pass the bus turnaround, and then the mountain centre. Just beyond the sharp left-hand bend into Cwm Ratgoed leave the road for a stony track on the left, continuing through the forest and parallel to the road.

Take the left fork opposite some tips and outbuildings (GR 774108) – the right fork crosses the Afon Ceiswyn towards the tips. This climbs steadily up the afforested slopes on the west side of Cwm Ratgoed. Ignore the path angling off right towards the fields of the valley bottom, but take the next waymarked path on the left. This climbs through the trees, crossing two more forestry roads before passing beneath the sparse crags of Mynydd y Waun and then emerging on a grassy enclo-sure on the south-east side of the Ceiswyn ridge.

An overgrown path winds up to a stile on the ridge, beyond which you turn right to climb to Mynydd Ceiswyn. The views to the mighty Cadair Idris crags are stunning – it's the first time on this route that the land-scape hasn't been dominated by spruce trees, although they're still below you on the right. The ridge walk continues by the fence all the way to Waun-oer's summit trig point.

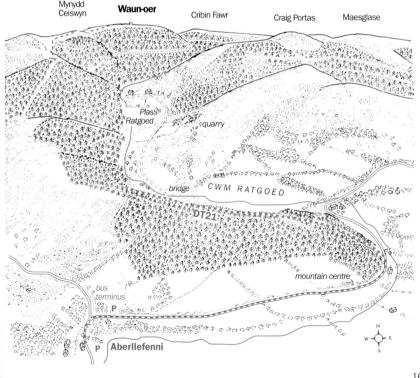

Other route options

You could follow Route DT21 through Cwm Ratgoed, but ignore the footpath turn-off and continue along the forest road towards the head of the valley beneath Waun-oer's eastern crags. Just before the stream crossing at GR 790150, climb left on a grassy rake through the trees to reach the col between Cribin Fawr and Waun-oer.

Now climb left on a steep path squeezing between the trees and the ridge fence. Note that the trees may eventually obscure this route and you'll have to cross the fence to climb along its other side.

RIDGE ROUTE

Cribin Fawr

Distance: ¾ mile/1.2km
Height gain: 295ft/90m
Time: ½ hour

Follow the ridge fence north-eastwards before taking a very steep path squeezing between the fence on the left and the trees. From a narrow col the path climbs back up the southern flanks of Cribin Fawr, where the hillscapes become more desolate and slightly more marshy.

Right: Descending Cribin Fawr's ridge towards Waun-oer.

Mynydd Fron-fraith, the bare hill of the mottled breast, is one of this book's smaller tops, but one well worth visiting for its great mountain views. It faces Cadair Idris across the Bala rift valley and you can look straight into Cadair's great tarn-filled, craggy corrie, Cwm Cau, and also along the length of Llyn Mwyngil to Tal-y-llyn.

Mynydd Fron-fraith is steep-sided and largely grassy in the summit area, but in the north its sides are sculpted with the impressive cliffs and gullies of Craig y Llam. The path to the summit traces the edge of the cliffs, offering some spectacular views of the valley below. You're so busy looking across to Cadair that you don't notice the conifers of the Llefenni valley to the east, but they're quite extensive.

An old highway climbs away from the A487 Tywyn road over the east shoulder of the hill before descending to Aberllefenni. Used these days by walkers and cyclists, it was once tramped by Roman soldiers and was part of their Sarn Helen highway, crossing Wales from north to south.

Opposite: Craig y Llam.
Right: The intimate view of Cwm Cau on Cadair Idris from Mynydd Fron-fraith.

Route DT22
Cwm Rhwyddfor and Craig y Llam
A walk with a fine view
Start: Roadside car park near the top of
    Cwm Rhwyddfor (GR: SH 753136)
Distance: 2¼ miles/3.5km
Height gain: 820ft/250m
Time: 1½ hours

Go over the stile opposite the car park and turn left across grassland parallel to the road. On reaching another roadside stile follow the path up to the right, climbing a stony gully north of Craig y Llam's rocky buttresses.

As the ground levels out the path becomes fainter and traverses wet, rushy ground to meet the now-tarred Roman road known as Sarn Helen. Turn right along this for about 100 paces then fork off to the right, up to the ridge crest. Now a fine little path follows the crest, offering stunning views across the face of Craig y Llam and the rift valley dominated on the far side by the southern flanks of mighty Cadair Idris.

Straddle the cross-fence and angle left across the rough heather which predominates on the far side, before following faint paths alongside a plantation of pine trees. Where a shallow grassy hollow opens out half-right, take a detour down it for a few paces – from here you'll get a fine view of Tal-y-llyn and its beautiful lake known to the Welsh as Llyn Mwyngil.

Continue by the fence to the grassy summit of Mynydd Fron-fraith, where you'll see Cadair Idris at its very best.

Descent

I would recommend going back the same way you came, but if you want to make a circular of it, descend WSW down steep grassy slopes to the field boundary marked on the map at GR 743115. This is in fact a partially-dismantled wall which often disappears beneath a thick cloak of bracken.

Follow it down to the right until you can see a bracken-free passage down to a green track below. Turn right along the track but watch out for a prominent crag on the left – it has a rowan growing out of it and a cross-wall running alongside. Just beyond the crag descend to a wall, which is the division between access land and so called cultivated land.

Follow this to the right to cross Nant y Benglog, then descend left down rough steep slopes, keeping the falls shown on the map just to the left. The way on to the road at the bottom of the falls is barred by a few gorse bushes, but it is possible. Turn left along the road – take care here for the traffic is often fast.

Leave the road for the campsite track on the right, then climb north-eastwards on the track up Cwm Rhwyddfor. This will lead you back to the car park.

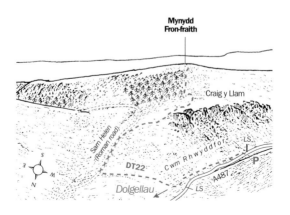

Opposite: Llyn Mwyngil and Tal-y-llyn from Mynydd Fron-fraith.

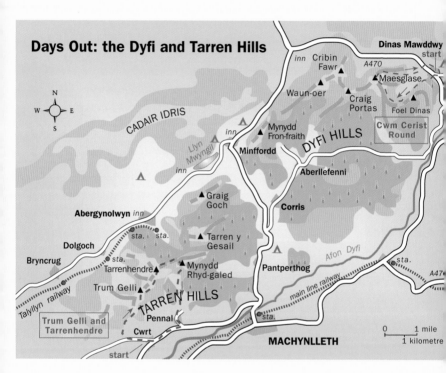

Days Out: the Dyfi and Tarren Hills

Dinas Mawddwy
start

inn Cribin Fawr

A470

▲Maesglase

Waun-oer

Craig Portas

Foel Dinas

▲

Cwm Cerist Round

CADAIR IDRIS

inn

Llyn Mwyngil

▲Mynydd Fron-fraith

DYFI HILLS

Minffordd

inn

Aberllefenni

Corris

▲Graig Goch

Abergynolwyn *inn*

Dolgoch

sta. sta.

▲Tarren y Gesail

Bryncrug

Tarrenhendre▲

Trum Gelli▲

sta.

▲Mynydd Rhyd-galed

Pantperthog

Afon Dyfi

sta.

A47

Talyllyn railway

TARREN HILLS

Trum Gelli and Tarrenhendre

Pennal

Cwrt

start

main line railway

sta.

MACHYNLLETH

0	1 mile
	1 kilometre

Days Out: the Dyfi and Tarren Hills

Trum Gelli, Tarrenhendre and Mynydd Rhyd-galed

Follows highways once travelled by pilgrims, traders and maybe even Roman soldiers

Start/finish: Cwrt car park (GR: SH 688002)
Distance: 12 miles/19km
Total height gain: 2460ft/750m
Time: 6–7 hours

The finest Tarren routes begin from the south by the meandering banks and cow pastures of the Dyfi. The best of these begins at Cwrt, a hamlet 4 miles/6.5km west of Machynlleth. It involves 5 miles/8km of superb ridge walking and substitutes the Christmas trees of the north with pleasing pastured hillsides, woodlands of oak and fresh, rushing streams.

From the car park at Cwrt, leave the main road for a little tarmac lane climbing westwards and giving glimpses of Cwm Ffernol between the surrounding wooded foothills. By the farmhouse at Pant-yr-on, the lane should be left for a stony track on the right which winds and climbs among rocky knolls. As the track gains height it gives views across the green fields of Cwm Maethlon (happy valley) to Llyn Barfog (bearded lake), a rushy hilltop tarn.

The track reaches a gate situated on a high saddle of moorland with the slopes of Allt Gwyddgwion to the right. Do not go through the gate here but look across to Allt Gwyddgwion to locate the ribbon of green which is the path. It begins beyond a primitive stile in the fence in the mid distance (GR 649004). (Ignore the faint track that goes through a gate in this fence as this just pussyfoots on the lower slopes and ends at a sheep pen.)

Beyond the stile a good sunken path develops and rakes across the hillside to reach the first huge Bronze Age cairn on Trum Gelli. Now you have wonderful views across the Dyfi Estuary, which more often than not will take on the appearance of a glistening silvery snake, slithering between the green fields of the valley to the flat coastal marshes of Borth. Pale hills across the Dyfi rise to Pumlumon Fawr (Plynlimon), perhaps the best-known hill in Mid Wales, and the birthplace of the mighty Severn and Wye.

The wide track continues on the right side of the ridge – good if you want shelter from any Atlantic winds, but bad for views. It's best to follow the ridge fence past the second cairn, another dating back to the Bronze Age.

The ridge bends to the right. The next hill is Tarren Cwm-ffernol. Here the terrain changes from grass to heather and moss and, as with most hills covered with such vegetation, the ground gains a certain amount of squelch.

The track becomes a path as bootprints scatter to miss the dark peaty pools. Tarrenhendre now takes centre-stage. Convenient

Above: Walking along the Tarren Cwm-ffernol ridge with the east cairn on Trum Gelli ahead.

ladder stiles straddle the cross walls, and a new deep valley appears to the left. This is the upper cwm of Dolgoch. The cluster of trees that you'll see at the far end hides the Dolgoch Falls, a popular tourist attraction, and well worth a visit on another day.

The ridge bends north on the final slopes to Tarrenhendre. There's an intersection of fences at the summit but no trig point or cairn for the peak-baggers among us to touch. However, across the tussocky grass and sparse heather there's the south face of Cadair Idris to admire. You've had glimpses of it for a while, but now you can see it in its entirety, with its southern cwms forming shadows in the cliffs.

Turn right from the summit to follow the fence-line eastwards down the slopes of Pant Gwyn. Now a new scene unfolds – a valley filled with spruce and larch trees. Their spread reaches almost to the craggy fringe of Tarrenhendre's east face.

The valley you're looking at is Nant Gwernol, sometimes referred to as the Wild Ravine. At one time this place would have echoed with the sounds of industry. But now a blanket of forestry has covered the extensive slate mines and quarries of Bryn Eglwys.

The rapidly expanding forest is also creeping up the sides of the ridge you're walking on, but the path is still clear and on open grassland. The highest hill of the group, Tarren y Gesail, now dominates the surroundings, but it's out on a limb to the north of the ridge.

In the col before the unnamed peak at GR 699043, look out for a track on the right, which will continue the descent. It joins a flinty track by some sheep enclosures, then swings to the right beneath the rocky sides of Mynydd Rhyd-galed.

At a sharp left-hand bend, leave the track for a path on the right, which begins beyond a ladder stile. Descend southwards down a trackless grassy spur, keeping on the west side of Mynydd Cefn-caer – a ladder stile in the cross-fence aids route-finding. Beyond this, veer away from the fence on the right to cross a rocky knoll. This way you will pick up the track that begins by another ladder stile and gate, which lie on the east side of the ridge.

The new track ends by a forest corner on Esgair Uchaf. Descend SSE down the pas-tured spur to the bottom fence of the field, then turn left to locate a track threading through gorse to a stream. Do not cross at the footbridge here, but turn right on a track high above the tree-lined stream. A yellow way-mark arrow on the right shows the point where the track should be abandoned for a parallel path, which stays above the nearby farmhouse at Esgair-isaf.

The path rejoins the farm track beyond the farmhouse and follows it down the hillside to cross the Afon Pennal on a new concrete bridge. Turn right along a pleasant country lane that ambles between hedgerow and pasture into Pennal village and the main road. A right turn along the road will lead back to the car park at Cwrt.

Below: Looking down from the Tarren ridge to the Dyfi Valley at Pennal.

The Cwm Cerist Round

*Another route on highways once travelled
by pilgrims, traders and maybe Roman
soldiers*

Start/finish: Dinas Mawddwy village car park
(GR: SH 859150)

Distance: 7 miles/11.2km

Total height gain: 2300ft/700m

Time: 4 hours

From the car park, turn right into the village and climb to the right on the lane to the busy A470 road. Turn right here but leave the road for a signed forestry footpath beginning at some steps on the far side of a lay-by at GR 855149. The clear path climbs through the trees of the lower slopes of Foel Dinas to a flinty forestry track.

After turning right along the track for about 50 yards/m, another waymark highlights the continuing partially stepped path, which zig-zags steeply uphill. After angling right (west) the cwm comes to more steps, which again climb steeply to a step stile on the edge of the moor.

The path climbs alongside the forest's top edge to enter the deep glaciated cwm of Maesglase, fringed at its head with precipitous crags, down which tumble two water-falls, the more spectacular being the one on the right, which has cut a rocky ravine through the best of the crags.

The narrow path cuts its way across steep flanks of grass, bilberry and bracken. Beyond a ladder stile, the going gets rougher with patches of gorse, thick bracken and heather crowding the path. This eases as you reach the pass of Bwlch Siglen, at the western edge of the cliffs. Another steep climb begins.

Follow the right-hand of two paths, which winds through thickets of bilberry closer to the stream than the forest edge. The path gradually veers left above the stream and for a short while you'll feel you're on the Pennine moors rather than in Snowdonia. But soon Maesglase's crags peep over the grasses and the route regains its momentum.

The path descends to ford the stream above the falls and passes by a huge domed rock offering fine views of the falls, which plummet down a nick in the near-vertical crags. The climb continues on a narrow grass path, which for most of the time stays fairly close to the cliff-edge, to Maesglase's first summit. By now there are wonderful views back to the Arans.

The path veers left along the northern edge and climbs gradually to the summit of Maen Du, where there's a small cairn with a stubby pole sticking out. The slightly higher summit above Craig Rhiw-erch lies to the west. It has an even smaller pile of stones hiding in the heather and tussocky grass.

Now return to Maen Du and descend the steep northern spur with a fence on your left as your guide.

Note: the winding path shown on OS Explorer maps does exist on the ground, just, but is hard to locate from above.

As the ridge levels out before the small rise to the next peak, Moel Cwm yr Eglwys (the hill of church valley), leave it for a rush-lined

Above: Craig Maesglase and the falls.
Overleaf: Bwlch Siglen at the head of Cwm Maesglase.

but firm grass track raking slightly right on slopes above Cwm yr Eglwys. This eventually enters farm pastures and comes down to the farm at Ty'n-y-celyn.

Go through a gate on the left side of the farmhouse, and turn left before continuing along the access drive to reach the busy A470 road. Cross the road, turn left for a short way, then go to the right along a narrow country lane running parallel with the main road. Take the left fork lane as you draw level with Nant Maesglase's cwm, before taking the right fork lane. This continues south-east along the lower slopes of Foel Benddin to the cottage of Y Pentre.

Take the upper, left fork by the cottage on an old track lined by rhododendrons, at the base of a forestry plantation. Watch out for a gate on the right just before a metal gate across the track. This marks the start of a grassy footpath angling downhill towards a caravan site. The path meets a more prominent path. Turn left along it and go through the lower (right) of two gates. The path soon follows a hedge on the left before descending through another gate to reach the camp-site drive near to its junction with the Dinas Mawddwy–Bala lane. Turn right along the lane, which passes through the village to return to the car park.

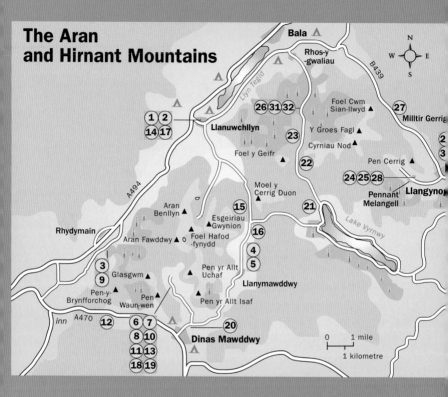

The Aran
and Hirnant Mountains

Bala

Rhos-y-gwaliau

Llyn Tegid

Llanuwchllyn

Foel Cwm Sian-llwyd ▲

Milltir Gerrig

Y Groes Fagl ▲

Cyrniau Nod ▲

Foel y Geifr ▲

Pen Cerrig ▲

Pennant Melangell

Llangyno

Moel y Cerrig Duon ▲

Lake Vyrnwy

Aran Benllyn ▲

Esgeiriau Gwynion ▲

Rhydymain

Aran Fawddwy ▲

Foel Hafod -fynydd

Pen yr Allt Uchaf ▲

Llanymawddwy

Glasgwm ▲

Pen-y-Brynfforchog ▲

Pen Waun-wen ▲

Pen yr Allt Isaf ▲

inn A470

Dinas Mawddwy

0   1 mile
1 kilometre

① ②
⑭ ⑰

㉖㉛㉜

㉓

㉒

㉗

②
③

㉔㉕㉘

㉑

⑮

⑯

④
⑤

③
⑨

⑫ ⑥ ⑦
⑧ ⑩
⑪ ⑬
⑱ ⑲

⑳

A494

B439

Blustery 35mph winds, snow flurries and temperatures of -5°C – that's what the weatherman had promised. I had intended to park the campervan on Bwlch y Groes, a high moorland pass between Bala and the Dyfi Valley. Imagining a dismal daybreak with the van doors glazed with ice and frozen shut until the heater had been on at least an hour, I copped out and telephoned one of my favourite B&Bs, Ty Derw at Dinas Mawddwy. Of course this was all done for the comfort of my wife, you understand!

THE PEAKS

Main Tops	height	
Aran Fawddwy	2969ft	905m
Aran Benllyn	2901ft	885m
Glasgwm	2538ft	774m
Foel Hafod-fynydd	2260ft	689m
Pen y Brynfforchog	2246ft	685m
Esgeiriau Gwynion	2200ft	671m
Cyrniau Nod	2187ft	667m
Y Groes Fagl	2161ft	659m
Foel Cwm Sian-llwyd	2125ft	648m
Foel y Geifr	2053ft	626m
Moel y Cerrig Duon	2050ft	625m
Pen yr Allt Uchaf	2020ft	616m
Pen Waun-wen	1974ft	602m
Pen yr Allt Isaf	1826ft	557m
Pen Cerrig	1623ft	495m

So, after a breakfast of smoked salmon and rosti, here we were in Llanymawddwy, plump with multi-layers of winter clothing. The snow flurries hadn't arrived. Instead the morning sun was strong, highlighting the reds of the hillside bracken and umbers of the heather, and casting long shadows into the deep cwms. Beautiful oak and birch woodland surrounds the Afon Dyfi, whose valley is surrounded by velvety, rounded hills, not unlike the Howgills of Cumbria.

I'd chosen to follow the map's little green dots which lead up to Pistyll Gwyn. The waterfalls were as good as they promised to be, and splashed over 100ft/30m from a notch on the horizon down a gigantic slab of rock. An exciting narrow path raked up the steep cwm-end slopes to the top of the falls. Here the green dots ended and, before the CROW Act, you would have had to turn back, for access to the Aran ridge was strictly forbidden. Aran farmers had formed a society whose aim was to restrict walkers' movements. So there were no paths to ease the way to the ridge.

Up on the next hill, Gwaun Lydan, I was reminded of the Forest of Bowland by peat hags and biscuit-coloured tussocky grasses. However, peeping over the distant moorland were the dark angular crags of the Aran ridge. A fence-line ran all the way to the ridge; otherwise this was pristine, erosion-free country, courtesy of those lovely Aran farmers – thanks, boys!

Gwaun Lydan leads to Drysgol, where you cannot but be captivated by Aran Fawddwy's tremendous volcanic cliffs, which throw black shadows across Creiglyn Dyfi, a sullen tarn that is birthplace to the river which shares its name. In no time we'd reached the trig point on the summit, which was dusted with snow but not enough to rob the rocks of their lovely gold and grey hues. As usual I had extracted the last seconds of light out of the day and had to make haste along the ridges, taking in another secretive waterfall and the fiery light playing among the February bracken and crags. This is truly God's country.

Spanning some 10 miles/16km from Llanuwchllyn on the southern shores of Llyn Tegid to the Dyfi valley at Dinas Mawddwy, the Aran mountains form a natural barrier between North and Mid Wales. In fact the Arans have always been a frontier range.

The names of the highest two peaks, Aran Benllyn and Aran Fawddwy, refer to the ancient cantrefs (hundreds) of Penllyn and Mawddwy, once strongholds of the kingdom of Powys. Penllyn's seat was the castle of Tomen y Bala, now just a grassy mound in the centre of Bala village. In 1202 Llewelyn the Great overran the castle with the troops of Elis ap Madog, the Lord of Penllyn, and after an emphatic victory, handed his lands to the Princes of Gwynedd in the north.

The Arans are also the southern boundary of Snowdonia's great ring of fire, formed by flows of volcanic lava and ash. As on Snowdon, glaciation has played a magnificent part in sculpting the mountains. There's a splendid 5 miles/8km of cliffs, gullies and rocky bluffs to scramble down and up, lots of little pools and ever-changing views into little cwms nobody has visited for years. Now, if you wish, you can pick your way between the crags down to the secretive Llyn Lliwbran, or check out the

Above: Aran Benllyn and Aran Fawddwy tower over Llyn Tegid.

ridge top north of Moel Ffenigl – the old permissive path used to divert to the west side from here. At one time locals believed that nearby Cadair Idris was a few feet higher and, jealous of its popularity, erected a huge cairn to redress the balance. Unfortunately, the visitors never materialised in the numbers they were hoping.

Although peaceful today, Dinas Mawddwy was not always so. In the sixteenth century it was terrorised by a band of thieves and murderers known as the Red Robbers of Mawddwy. The treacherous men were said to have red hair, hence their name, and lived in the region of Cwm Cywarch beneath Aran Fawddwy. Their exploits were known throughout the land, and travellers in Central Wales would make wide detours to avoid the likelihood of being attacked.

Dinas Mawddwy lay beneath the robbers' hideouts and terrified villagers would barricade themselves in at night. Little stopped these desperate criminals, however, and they continued their exploits of robbery and murder. It is reported that they openly drove stolen cattle across the county to sell at market.

Local ruler Baron Lewis Owen was commissioned by Queen Mary to bring the men to justice. On Christmas Eve 1553 his men surrounded the robbers' lair. Eighty men were captured and executed, but this was not the end to the business for survivors of the gang plotted their revenge. Knowing the route the baron regularly took to attend the local assizes they decided to ambush him and found the ideal situation at Llidiart y Barwyn (the Baron's Gate), 3 miles/4.8km east of Mallwyd, the next village to Dinas Mawddwy.

Here, in a wooded gorge, the road forded a stream and the baron would have to slow down. After felling some trees to block his progress further, the robbers hid behind some nearby rocks. The baron and his men arrived on cue and stopped to clear the obstructions. As they did so they were greeted with a shower of arrows. The baron was deserted by his escort and was immediately set upon, dragged from his horse and stabbed to death. Following this the remainder of the gang were hunted down. Most were executed but some fled the country.

In the middle of the nineteenth century that famed traveller George Borrow walked through the village from Bala. In his book *Wild Wales,* he noted that it was 'little more than a collection of huts . . . a squalid place'. He continued: 'I found it anything but silent and deserted. Fierce-looking red-haired men, who seemed if they might be descendants of the red-haired banditti of old, were staggering about and sounds of drunken revelry echoed from the huts.' These, he later learned, were the hard-working, hard-drinking men of the local lead and slate mining fraternities.

Until 1959 Dinas had a railway line, linking it with Machynlleth and Shrewsbury. The old station building is now a café, while the former engine shed houses the Meirion (woollen) Mill and Craft Centre.

Up-river from Dinas Mawddwy, the hamlet of Llanymawddwy lies beneath Bwlch y Groes, the pass of the cross. This used to be the stamping ground of St Tydecho, cousin of St Cadfan and one of three saints sent from Brittany in the sixth century to introduce Christianity to Wales. Hereabouts, they've renamed the Dyfi the Llaeth-nant (milk stream). The name may come from the fact that the waters are white with spray as they tumble down the valley from beneath Aran Fawddwy's crags in a series of cataracts and waterfalls, but Tydecho's name crops up in another explanation for it. The story goes that one day his maidservant returned from the mountain pastures sobbing that she had spilt all the milk while crossing the stream. As these were times of great poverty, Tydecho used his powers to convert the waters into milk so the villagers wouldn't go hungry.

In the north-east, the Hirnant ridges are again of thick heather and moorland in character. Several streams born on the north side flow down to Llyn Tegid and the Dee Valley. The main one, the Hirnant, is heavily afforested with spruce and larch, which extends to the 2000ft contour just below the tops. Forestry tracks allow dull but fast progress, as does the tarred public road linking Bala with the Vyrnwy Reservoir.

Cyrniau Nod is the highest of these eastern peaks, but perhaps the most accessible is Foel Cwm Sian-llwyd, which can be reached from Llangynog in the Tanat Valley to the south by way of Cwm Rhiwarth, a splendid crag-fringed pastoral glen with a fine waterfall plunging down from cliffs at its head. The poet Samuel Taylor Coleridge passed through Llangynog in 1794 on his way to Bala and noted that the Berwyn mountains were 'sublimely terrible: the water cold as ice and clear as infant diamonds as it plummeted down rugged stony clefts'.

Overleaf: Dyfi Valley mosaic from Darren Ddu.

Anyone who has stood on the shores of Bala's lake, Llyn Tegid, will remember the pyramidal peak that looks down from afar. The peak is impressive and it's made from volcanic Ordovician rock, lots of it. The mountain is Aran Benllyn, second highest of the range at 2901ft/885m. It rises erect in the middle of the Aran ridge at a point where the eastern flanks turn from rock-scattered slopes to shattered cliffs.

The name derives from the cantref (hundred) of Penllyn, which encompassed lands to the west as far as Gwynedd, a kingdom it was eventually conquered by in 1202.

Aran Benllyn has its own glacial tarn, Llyn Lliwbran, which is tightly tucked in a small but deep grassy cwm beneath its eastern cliffs. It's easy to pass along the ridge without even seeing this splendid tarn. Beneath this, two desolate spurs decline further to a plinth of rough moorland and down to the fields of Cwm Croes.

The ridge itself is stepped with crag and firm grassy terrain, studded with several shallow ridge-top pools, most unnamed but the largest known as Llyn Pen Aran, which lies to the north of the summit.

There are no quick routes to Aran Benllyn as parking in Cwm Croes is almost impossible without obstructing local farmers. Most walkers climb the ridge from Llanuwchllyn and return by walking the length of the valley using the lane back to Talardd on the Bwlch y Groes road.

Opposite: The cliffs of Aran Benllyn. Right: Llyn Pen Aran and Aran Benllyn.

Route AH1
Llanuwchyllyn and the North Ridge

A classic mountain ridge walk

Start: Car park at Pont y Pandy, Llanuwchllyn
   (GR: SH 879297)

Distance: 3¾ miles/6km

Height gain: 2395ft/730m

Time: 2½ hours

This route to the Arans begins over a ladder stile and on to a farm road by the bridge over the Afon Twrch. After a few hundred yards/metres, another signpost shows the way to the right across fields towards the ridge.

Numerous ladder stiles enable the crossing of drystone walls and fences as the path turns left at the foot of the ridge. In the lower regions the path keeps slightly to the west side of the ridge proper and thus views are restricted to the east. In views to the west the craggy face of the little-known peak Dduallt is the dominant feature, although behind you Bala's lake becomes increasingly visible beneath the long knobbly ridge you are climbing.

Eventually the path climbs left on the more craggy slopes of Moel Ffenigl. Now the route becomes more exciting, with more rock faces ahead, topped by the fierce crags of Aran Benllyn. On the rocky ridge overlooking Craig y Llyn keep a watch for the views down to Llyn Lliwbran, for it's tucked quite tightly in its cwm beneath the cliffs – you'll have to hop over the low fence to see it.

A few tiny ridge-top pools are passed (not marked on 1:50,000 maps) as the path climbs

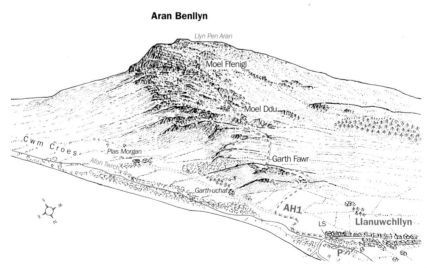

Aran Benllyn

Llyn Pen Aran

Moel Ffenigl

Moel Ddu

Cwm Croes

Plas Morgan

Afon Twrch

Garth Fawr

Garth-uchaf

AH1

LS

Llanuwchllyn

P

a series of rocky steps. After rounding the larger pool of Llyn Pen Aran, the path makes one final assault up to the boulder-scattered summit, which is topped by a large but low cairn.

Above: Climbing on the North Ridge route to Aran Benllyn.

Route AH2
Cwm Croes and Llyn Lliwbran

A fine route past a secluded cliff-shaded tarn
Start: Car park at Pont y Pandy, Llanuwchllyn
(GR: SH 879297)
Distance: 5¼ miles/8.5km
Height gain: 2525ft/770m
Time: 3½ hours

---

*Note: the field path from Nant-y-Llyn farm
in Cwm Croes to the edge of the access
land beneath Llyn Lliwbran uses a Tir Gofal
permissive path, which can be closed on
certain days. Dogs must be on leads and are
not allowed at all during lambing time.
These agreements come up for renewal
every ten years, so please do nothing to
prejudice their continuation.*

From Llanuwchllyn, the route heads for the
beautiful pastoral valley of Cwm Croes, and
the quickest way is by the Dinas Mawddwy
road to Pont Talardd, followed by the one up
Cwm Croes. There's a signed short-cut path
from the east bank of the Twrch to the Dinas
road at Pen-rhiw-Dwrch.

Alternatively, there is a perfectly feasible
route beginning on the farm lane by the
bridge over the Twrch (Pont y Pandy). This
ends at Plas Morgan, from where cross-field
paths lead to the Cwm Croes lane at Ty-mawr
farm. (See Days Out: Cwm Croes and the
Aran Ridge, page 287.)

Both routes then head south on the pretty
lane through Cwm Croes. Opposite Nant-
y-Llyn farm you turn right through a gate
and climb fields parallel to the Nant y Llyn
stream, which has cut a fine tree-filled gorge

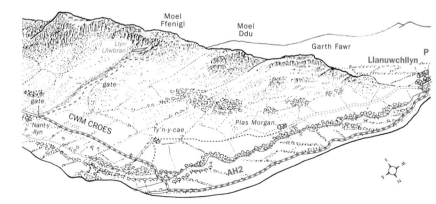

Opposite: Llyn Lliwbran from Aran Benllyn's North Ridge.

on the left. Occasional waymark posts and a faint vehicle track assure you of the way.

The path enters access land at a gate in a drystone wall. Once through it turn left and climb rough grassy hillsides still keeping parallel to the stream. On seeing the lake, climb the spur of Cefn Rhudd on the right. Now you can get a good elevated view of the lake and the severe cliffs at its head. You'll need to round those cliffs but it's easily done by angling slightly right as the ground steepens, to gain the more broken ground of rocky bluffs and grass to the north.

You should soon reach the ridge fence just south of Moel Ffenigl. Turn left alongside the fence to climb above the cliffs of Craig y Llyn. A steep, eroded scree path takes the route up to the pool of Llyn Pen Aran, beyond which the final climb to Aran Benllyn begins.

Descent

Note: only use this route in clear and clement conditions.

Descend north past Llyn Pen Aran and down the loose scree path to the ridge above Craig y Llyn. Although Llyn Lliwbran is just below you, the cliffs bar the way, so continue north towards Moel Ffenigl.

Just before the pull up to that summit, climb the low ridge fence on your right and go to the rim of the east slopes. If you're in the right place they should be safe and easy with plenty of grass and broken rock leading down to the spur of Cefn Rhudd. Descend the spur to the far end of the lake.

Note the crumbling wall by the outflow stream: these two features are your guides down the hillside. There's now a pathless descent parallel to the wall and stream.

Below: Descending to Nant-y-llyn farm in Cwm Croes.

Watch out for a gate in the wall at GR 883256 as it marks the start of the way-marked Tir Gofal route down the farm pastures ahead.

Faint vehicle tracks and the odd way-marker post guide you down to the roadside gate opposite the farm of Nant-y-llyn. Here you can turn left down the Cwm Croes lane to Pont Talardd, where you turn left for Llanuwchllyn.

Other route options

There is a Tir Gofal permissive route from the road-end at Dwrnudon just off the A494 south-west of Llanuwchllyn at GR 862282. It follows a track by a conifer plantation and above the east banks of the Afon Dwrnudon. Once in the access area you could follow the fence south-westwards to the ridge at Craig Geifr.

There's another Tir Gofal route further south-west with access from the A494 at Pont Fronwydd (GR 832246). This climbs on to the southern slopes of Foel Fach, where you can climb Foel Fawr on to Aran Benllyn.

RIDGE ROUTES

Foel Hafod-fynydd

Distance: 1¾ miles/2.8km
Height gain: 425ft/130m (1065ft/325m descent)
Time: ¾ hour

From the summit descend south along the path at first, but where the path skirts the western side of the next peak, Erw y Ddafad-ddu, follow the fence on the left and cross it to the east side of the ridge.

When you come to the wide grassy spur that divides those precipitous eastern crags, use it to descend towards the tarn, Creiglyn Dyfi. The spur takes you easily down to the bottom of the Foel Hafod-fynydd ridge, with views down the crag and grass of Cwm Llwydd and along the cliffs of Aran Benllyn.

Climb ENE up the grassy ridge. In the later stages you meet an acute fence corner. Follow the right-hand fence to the summit, which overlooks both Cwm Llwydd and the long, pastured valley of Cwm Croes.

Aran Fawddwy

Distance: 1¼ miles/2km
Height gain: 395ft/120m
Time: ¾ hour

A clear path runs south along a wide and stony ridge interspersed with rocky bluffs and boulders. There's a small rise and fall to an intermediate peak, Erw y Ddafad-ddu, before a steady climb to Fawddwy's peak.

ARAN FAWDDWY

The Aran's highest peak, Aran Fawddwy at 2969ft/905m is also the highest Welsh peak south of Snowdon, and it shows in its panoramas which extend to the Brecon Beacons in the south, the hazy foothills of the Marches to the east and Snowdon itself to the north.

Hidden behind Aran Benllyn when seen from Bala and the northern shoreline of Llyn Tegid, Aran Fawddwy impresses when seen on approaches from the south and east, although even here walkers will have to gain the outlying ridges to see its cliffs and that spectacular cwm where Creiglyn Dyfi gives birth to the river of the same name. As is the case with the whole range, when seen from the Wnion valley in the west, the mountain looks aloof, with its crags sparse and broken.

The summit is domed compared to Benllyn's angular shape and capped by a stone-built trig point. From here more than anywhere in the Aran you can see and feel the change from mountain to moor – from Ordovician to Silurian geology, and from Snowdonia to Mid Wales – for as you look down the grassy slopes of the upper Dyfi towards the land they call Mawddwy, the terrain changes to velvety-smooth, rounded hills.

Left: Aran Fawddwy and Creiglyn Dyfi from Drysgol.

Route AH3

Rhydymain and Waun Camddwr

An unspectacular but easy-paced route

Start: From the minor road near Rhydymain
    (GR: SH 813218). There's room for two
    carefully parked cars or, if full, by Esgair-
    gawr farm (GR: SH 816224)

Distance: 4¼ miles/7km

Height gain: 2460ft/750m

Time: 2½ hours

The track climbs from the south side of the lane just west of Lletty-wyn farm across high fields before entering a large spruce plantation marked Coed-y-Brenin on the OS Explorer map.

Take the main left fork forestry track, which soon runs parallel with the Afon Cwm-ochr.

At GR 828208, just before this main track doubles back, take the right fork which zig-zags up to the stile and gate at the forest's edge. From here you can see the pale crags of distant Aran Fawddwy on the skyline and the rugged if haphazard form of Glasgwm on the right.

A waymark post highlights the direction up the slope of Creigiau Brithion, through rushy moorland studded with rock knolls. The path veers left to reach the ridge fence and climbs steadily over the craggy mound of Waun Camddwr before tackling Aran Fawddwy. Soon you can look down the mountain's east-ern cliffs, which have been hiding behind these tamer western slopes. From the trig point you can just about see the tarn of Creig-lyn Dyfi, which hides beneath those cliffs.

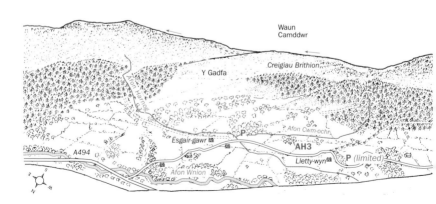

Above: On Aran Fawddwy's summit.

Route AH4

Llanymawddwy and Darren Ddu

A fine descent route with splendid views of the Dyfi Valley

Start: Llanymawddwy (GR: SH 903190)

Distance: 4¼ miles/7km

Height gain: 2540ft/775m

Time: 2½ hours

Turn right out of the parking area by the phone box, heading along the road towards Bwlch y Groes and Bala. On reaching Bryn Hall, turn left along a tarred farm lane to reach Brynuchaf farm.

Go through the gate to the left of the older of two farmhouses and climb the hillside on a track which eventually curves right and becomes more prominent. It skirts the edge of the rocky chasm on the spur of Darren Ddu before giving up on tussocky moorland. Now follow the fence across the peat and tussocks of Gwaun Lydan before continuing up the easier slopes of Drysgol, where you join the main Hengwm path from Cwm Cywarch.

This climbs over the narrow neck of Drws Bach, where a cairn was built by the RAF St Athan Mountain Rescue Team to commemorate Senior Aircraftsman Mike Aspain, who was killed by lightning while on a call-out in 1960.

From the cairn you follow the path across rockier ground on to Aran Fawddwy's south ridge, and over a stile where you follow a fence leading to the summit trig point.

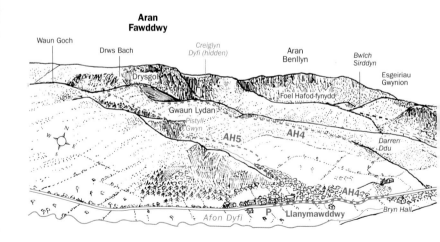

Descent

From the summit trig point, descend south-westwards on a cairned path along the boulder-scattered main ridge before veering south at a fence corner to Drws Bach, where there's a memorial cairn. The fence leads you on to a narrow neck with steep drops into the gigantic hollow of Hengwm on the right and on to Drysgol, where there's a fine grassy promenade.

After descending east to a fence intersection, you need to leave the main path and continue east then south-east by another fence on to Gwaun Lydan, where the grass becomes more tussocky but not horrendously so. The fence takes you down to the rocky gorge of Darren Ddu, where you'll find the clear track running along the south-west edge. This fine route takes you down to the Bala–Dinas Mawddwy road at Bryn Hall.

Below: The track between Darren Ddu and Llanymawddwy.

Route AH5

Llanymawddwy and Cwm Dyniewyd

Visiting superb waterfalls and some wild country

Start: Llanymawddwy (GR: SH 903190)

Distance: 4½ miles/7.3km

Height gain: 2560ft/780m

Time: 2½ hours

Follow the little lane opposite the car parking area, climbing from the church past stands of pine before winding into Cwm Dyniewyd. Now you can see up this long cwm to the distant waterfalls, with pastured hillsides to your right and the rougher bracken-clad slopes of Pen Foel-y-ffridd to the left.

Cross the stream just beyond a waterfall – there's a guide rail and huge boulder in the stream bed to help you across – and climb the far bank to join a path along pastures parallel to the river. The way steepens as it approaches the Pistyll Gwyn falls (this section will be difficult in wintry conditions).

Above the falls a faint path continues up a moorland valley by the edge of spruce woods to reach the pass between Waun Goch and Drysgol. Turn right and climb to the latter before continuing over the narrow neck of Drws Bach past the memorial cairn on to Aran Fawddwy's south ridge. Now a fence leads to the summit.

Descent

Descend (as on Route AH4) on the well-defined path heading south-eastwards to Drws Bach, then along the craggy narrow neck to Drysgol. Stay with the main path as it descends further down a grass ridge to the col beneath Waun Goch.

Here leave the main path to follow the north side of a fence descending south-west into the valley of Pumryd Fawr to the edge of a spruce plantation (GR 881203). Continue along the eastern edge of the plantation on a narrow path taking the route to the top of the Pistyll Gwyn waterfalls. Take care to locate the steep path to the left (north) of the falls.

This traverses rock-interspersed slopes at the head of Cwm Dyniewyd before heading down the valley (this section would be difficult in wintry conditions). Watch out for the river crossing, which is highlighted by a large boulder in the stream and a handrail by it. On the other side a good green track leads back to the valley at Llanymawddwy.

Above: Cwm Dyniewyd and the Pistyll Gwyn falls.

Route AH6
Cwm Cywarch and Hengwm

A pleasant if unspectacular route in the middle regions

Start: Cwm Cywarch (GR: SH 853187)
Distance: 5½ miles/9km
Height gain: 2625ft/800m
Time: 3½ hours

Cwm Cywarch is magnificent, with towering buttresses of crag to the west contrasting with velvety green hills to the east. On the first stages of the walk you turn your back on the crags for a while and head for those more verdant hillsides.

From the car park turn left up the lane for a few paces then turn right on a signed footpath, which crosses a footbridge over the Afon Cywarch before climbing on a rough track by trees and hedges. Turn left along the farm track raking across the hillslopes into Hengwm, a beautiful deep cwm hemmed in on all sides by verdant but steep-sided mountains. The path now rakes up the grassy hillslopes on the right and heads towards the end of the cwm.

On reaching a marshy col at the head of the cwm, turn left on a path climbing mostly alongside a ridge fence to the summit of Drysgol. Here the view northwards becomes

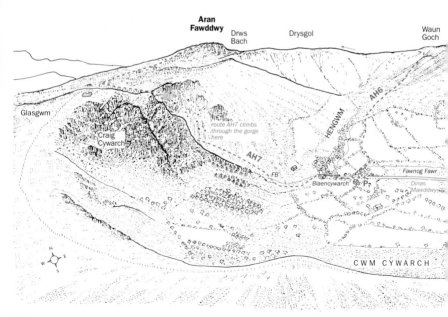

spectacular, with the craggy dome and cliffs of Aran Fawddwy soaring from the waters of Creiglyn Dyfi, one of the best-situated tarns in southern Snowdonia. The outflow of the lake – the infant Afon Dyfi but hereabouts known as the Llaethnant – plummets down a narrow rocky gorge into a hollow beneath the grassy flanks of Foel Hafod-fynydd.

Now the ridge turns westwards and becomes narrow and craggier, climbing along Drws Bach, where you pass the memorial cairn to an RAF Mountain Rescue volunteer before continuing up the rocky slopes to Aran Fawddwy's main ridge. Here you join the path from Cywarch and Rhydymain. It's now just a short promenade to the stone-built summit trig point.

Route AH7
Craig Cywarch

The most spectacular route in the Arans
Start: Cwm Cywarch (GR: SH 853187)
Distance: 4¾ miles/6km
Height gain: 2590ft/790m
Time: 3 hours

Walk to the end of the road and along the continuing track past Blaencywarch farm. A waymarked grass ribbon of a path cuts through the bracken and boulders beneath Craig Cywarch and up into the gorge beyond. Cross the stream on a footbridge and keep to the right side of the stream, which splashes down in white-water torrents.

The path climbs to the more open ground of a grassy upland cwm, where it follows a fence past a couple of shallow pools to a pass. Here you should turn right alongside the ridge fence. Sullen and peaty at first, once over the subsidiary peak (marked as Waun Camddwr on the OS map), the going improves, and soon the path is climbing boldly across firm grass and rock outcrops to reach Aran Fawddwy's summit trig point.

Left: Climbing out of Cwm Cywarch.

Other route options

There is an often-used route from the car parking area by Esgair Gawr (GR 816224) climbing east through the conifers surrounding the Afon Harnog. Beyond the forest the route gets rough and pathless on tussocky grass and heather.

You could also access the mountain by way of Llanymawddwy in the east and the Llaethnant (upper Dyfi) valley before climbing to Creiglyn Dyfi (lake) and the grass spur of Erw y Ddafad-ddu, but there would be a difficult stream crossing at the entrance of Ceunant y Briddell, and the terrain by the Llaethnant river is very rough and marshy.

Below: The path from Drws Bach to Aran Fawddwy.

RIDGE ROUTES

Aran Benllyn

Distance: 1¼ miles/2km
Height gain: 310ft/95m
Time: ¾ hour

From the trig point a good path heads north descending steeply over boulder-strewn terrain, before crossing a ladder stile to the west side of the fence. An easy climb follows to the cairn topping the middle peak, Erw y Ddafad-ddu, easily recognised by the break in the cliffs for a gracefully arced grassy spur, which declines to the tarn of Creiglyn Dyfi. On descending from this peak the ridge narrows and the cliffs resume on the east side as the path makes the final climb to Aran Benllyn's summit.

Foel Hafod-fynydd

Distance: 1¾ miles/2.8km
Height gain: 395ft/120m (1115ft/340m
   descent)
Time: 1 hour

From the trig point descend north along the bouldery ridge but, rather than following the path along the high western side of Erw y Ddafad-ddu, stay with the ridge fence until you reach the top of a wide grassy spur declining eastwards towards the tarn of Creiglyn Dyfi.

The steep course is south-easterly at first, changing to southerly as the spur narrows. The views down Cwm Llwydd on your left and the cliffs of Aran Benllyn and Aran Fawddwy are sublime, with the tarn capturing centre-stage.

At the base of the spur turn left (eastwards) to climb the ridge of Foel Hafod-fynydd. In the later stages you meet an acute fence corner. Follow the right-hand fence to the summit, which now overlooks both Cwm Llwydd and the long pastured valley of Cwm Croes.

Glasgwm

Distance: 2¾ miles/4.4km
Height gain: 755ft/230m
Time: 1½ hours

Follow the fence-side path south-westwards down bouldery ground, ignoring the left fork path which descends to Drysgol. The ridge becomes ill-defined and broad, but the fence still guides the route down, over the subsidiary peak of Waun Camddwr. Beyond this the going gets a little wetter in places, but not excessively so.

The path arrives at a crossing with the path straddling the ridge on its course from Cwm Cywarch to Rhydymain. Glasgwm's rock and grass slopes now rear up ahead. Stay on the west side of the fence to climb on easy gradients. In the upper stages the grass gives way to scree but soon you're at the summit cairn looking across the large tarn, Llyn y Fign.

Pen yr Allt Uchaf

Distance: 2¾ miles/4.5km
Height gain: 245ft/75m
Time: 1¾ hours

From the trig point, head south-west along the rocky ridge. Go left at the ladder stile in the ridge fence at GR 859220 and descend southwards down craggy slopes. Over another stile the path continues its descent by a fence to the memorial cairn at Drws Bach, where there are precipitous drops into the deep chasm of Hengwm.

Continue eastwards beyond the fence on a now grassy ridge over Drysgol, where the path descends south-east to a boggy col at the head of Hengwm. From the col, don't descend with the main path into Hengwm but instead climb south to the soggy summit of Waun Goch. A broad ridge now leads south-west to a ladder stile in a fence intersection, beyond which the highest summit lies.

Slightly off the beaten track of the main Aran ridge, Gwaun y Llwyni, which means the moor of the grove, is a splendid and very worthwhile peak with a fine craggy fringe and precipitous slopes encircling the cavernous green hollow of Hengwm.

The southern slopes are precipitous but largely grassy except for those overlooking the cascading Camddwr steam. Here slopes of heather, outcropping crag, scree and bracken face the great buttresses of Craig Cywarch across a deep ravine. On these lower slopes is the stone mountaineers' hut, Bryn Hafod, surely one of the most austere and spectacularly sited buildings in Snowdonia.

Route AH8
Cwm Cywarch

A spectacular route taking in crags and clifftops

Start: Cwm Cywarch (GR: SH 853187)
Distance: 2¾ miles/4.4km
Height gain: 1870ft/570m
Time: 2 hours

Turn left out of the car park and walk to the end of the road and along the continuing track past Blaencywarch farm. A waymarked grass ribbon of a path cuts through the bracken and boulders beneath the magnificent buttresses and craggy ramparts of Craig Cywarch and into a spacious cwm. Cross the stream on a footbridge and turn left with the path.

Opposite: Gwaun y Llwyni seen across the valley at Blaen Cywarch.
Below: Starting out from Blaen Cywarch with Gwaun y Llwyni on the right.

The path follows the main stream, which is soon confined by a rocky gorge in which it tumbles and splashes in a series of impressive waterfalls. The winding path keeps well to the right of it before reaching a wild grassy upper cwm. Stay with the path alongside a wire fence to an intersection with the main ridge fence at a moorland col.

Go over the step stile in the ridge fence and turn right following the path climbing towards Aran Fawddwy. It straddles the minor top of Waun Camddwr, where you'll see the hollow of the Camddwr stream on your right – this discourages you from making a beeline for Gwaun y Llwyni's summit.

Where the hollow becomes shallower beyond two fence intersections, and where the main fence kinks to the left, leave the main path and head eastwards towards a rocky tor on the col between Drws Bach and Gwaun y Llwyni. Skirt around the tor to reach a path on the far side of the crest.

Follow this to the right as it traces the rim of spectacular crags that encircle the head of Hengwm. A wonderful cliff-top route now heads south to the tiny pile of slates capping Gwaun y Llwyni's summit.

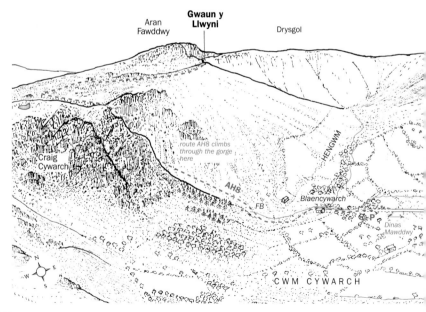

Other route options

You could divert from Route AH8 at the foot-bridge at GR 850197 and strike up the hill-side by the banks of the Camddwr stream, which plummets from Waun Camddwr. While this is a direct and more satisfactory approach to the summit, it is very rough, especially in summer when the heather and the bracken will impede your progress.

You could also take the popular path into Hengwm, then climb to Drysgol and Drws Bach, before swinging left on a fine cliff-top path to the summit. It would seem strange to list this as a primary route to our hill, as Drws Bach is much higher than Gwaun y Llwyni, but it could be part of a circular tour taking in Glasgwm and Craig Cywarch. The path from Esgair Gawr above Rhydymain meets Route AH8 at the col south of Waun Camddwr.

RIDGE ROUTE

Aran Fawddwy

Distance: 1½ miles/2.5km
Height gain: 200ft/ 60m
Time: ¾ hour

This spectacular route follows a narrow path hugging the craggy rim of Hengwm, which it encircles before reaching the memorial cairn on Drws Bach. Here you join the Hengwm Drysgol path (Route AH6), which climbs NNW across bouldery ground, by the fence at first.

Beyond a ladder stile in the fence the path climbs Fawddwy's bouldery upper slopes to the south cairn before continuing along the main ridge fence to the trig point, which lies a short way to the right.

Below: Gwaun y Llwyni (right) showing the terrain to be crossed from the pass below to the summit.

Glasgwm has borrowed its name from a wild grassy corrie to the north-west, for its name means the blue or green corrie. This is a mountain of some girth and, while it may not be the highest Aran, it has the most splendid crags in the range.

Craig Cywarch, as they are collectively known, totally dominate the valley, the hard rock buttresses and shadowy gullies offering a complete contrast to the verdant pastoral scenery below. This is a place for climbers, but walkers can also enjoy intimate views of the crag from two routes: one an old quarry track, which happily has now melded into its surroundings; the other, an ancient traders' path, which winds up the head of the cwm to the ridge.

The summit is expansive and largely grassy, with two separate tops. A large cairn caps the slightly lower east summit, while the western one, studded with a little rock, is otherwise featureless. There are also two lakes: Llyn Bach lies to the north and has a pleasant pebbly bed, while the larger Llyn y Fign lies to the south in a shallow grassy basin.

As with many Aran peaks the west slopes of Glasgwm are featureless and drab: a mix of heather mosses, rough grassland and sparse crag, now partially cloaked with spruce and larch. These more gentle slopes and forestry tracks do however offer reasonable ways to the top.

Opposite: Glasgwm's eastern crags.
Below: Glasgwm from the north across the Wnion valley.

Route AH9
Rhydymain and Waun Camddwr

An unspectacular but easy-paced route

Start: From minor road near Rhydymain
(GR: SH 813218). There is room for two
carefully parked cars or, if full, by Esgair-
gawr farm (GR: SH 816224)

Distance: 4¼ miles/7km

Height gain: 1920ft/585m

Time: 2½ hours

From the car park walk south-westwards along the lane until you see a footpath on the left, signed to Cywarch. This follows a track climbing across high fields before entering a large spruce plantation marked Coed-y-Brenin on the OS Explorer map.

Take the main left fork forestry track, which soon runs parallel with the Afon Cwm-ochr.

At GR 828208, just before this main track doubles back, take the right fork, which zig-zags up to the stile and gate at the forest's edge. From here you can see the pale crags of distant Aran Fawddwy on the skyline and the rugged if haphazard form of Glasgwm on the right.

A waymark post highlights the direction up the slope of Creigiau Brithion and through rushy moorland studded with rock knolls. On reaching the fence at the marshy col, turn right and climb on the much firmer terrain of Glasgwm's northern slopes. The climb is steady over grass studded with crag, and soon you reach the cairned east top, which over-looks the large tarn of Llyn y Fign and the smaller Llyn Bach. The slightly higher west summit lies just a little bit further along the fence-line.

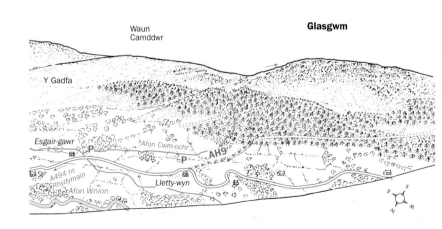

Above: The climb from Rhydymain path to Waun Camddwr.

Route AH10
Blaen Cywarch

A magnificent route beneath the crags of
Cwm Cywarch

Start: Cwm Cywarch (GR: SH 853187)

Distance: 2 miles/3.2km

Height gain: 2085ft/635m

Time: 1½ hours

Turn left out of the car park to follow the tarred road to its terminus. Follow the succeeding track signed to Rhydymain, alongside the stream and past Blaencywarch farm, with immense crags towering ahead and to the left.

Bryn Hafod, the little stone building on the hillside ahead, is a climbers' club hut. Before you reach it leave the track for a ladder stile on the left. The path now climbs into a craggy cwm overshadowed by the slopes of Creigiau Camddwr.

It crosses the stream on a footbridge and continues up the cwm. The main stream is soon confined by a rocky gorge, where it tumbles and splashes in impressive waterfalls. The winding path keeps well to the right of it before reaching a shallow grass-and-rock upper cwm.

Stay with the path alongside a wire fence to an intersection with the main ridge fence

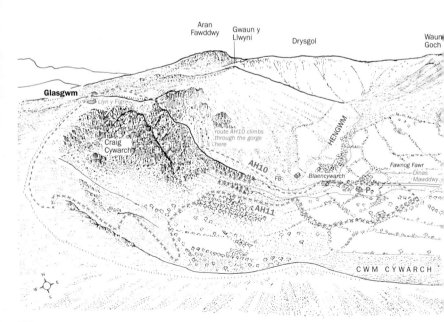

at a moorland col. Go over a step stile in the ridge fence here before turning left, uphill, by the fence to climb the easy gradients of Glasgwm's northern slopes. In the upper stages the grass gives way to scree but soon you're at the summit cairn looking across the large tarn, Llyn y Fign.

Route AH11
Cwm Cywarch and the south ridge

*Another stunning route following an old
quarry track*

Start: Cwm Cywarch (GR: SH 853187)
Distance: 2¾ miles/4.4km
Height gain: 2100ft/640m
Time: 2¼ hours

Turn right out of the car park and follow the road back to an open area of land. Here a stony vehicle track angles right to ford a stream (this can be difficult after heavy rain) and continues past the cottage of Gesail and a ruin beyond it.

Below: Descending the old quarry track into Cwm Cywarch.

Note: the right of way marked on the map hasn't existed on the ground for many a year and has been replaced in practice with the track you're on. It would have crossed the horrible field of rushes you see half-left and continued on a narrow spur between two streams – this is now choked with head-high bracken.

Continue with the track as it zigzags beneath spectacular rock-faces. There's great beauty here in the contrasts between the magnificent rock scenery and the soft green fields, hedgerow and velvety slopes of the hills on the other side of the valley.

The drama of the scene subsides as the track reaches the col. Turn right here and go over the step stile near a fence intersection. Don't cross the adjacent ladder stile but follow the narrow path near the cliff edge.

Note: in bad ice, snow or mist follow the fence until GR 837188, where it turns left, then head north to the summit.

The path climbs north to the summit lake, Llyn y Fign. Go over the stile in the fence to the right of the lake and continue north for the summit cairn.

Descent

In normal conditions head south, keeping to the left of the lake before descending on a path above the cliffs of Craig Cywarch. Go over a step stile above the col beneath the slopes of Y Gribin, and follow a path half-left to reach the top of a wide track.

This zigzags down into Cwm Cywarch with tremendous views of the crags and valley beyond. Note that the marked right of way descending from GR 847180 doesn't exist on the ground so stay with the track, which winds down the mountainside to pass the cottage of Gesail. The track fords the Afon Gelli and comes to the main valley road south of the main car park.

Note: descent in wintry conditions: check before starting off on your round that the Afon Gelli is fordable. From the summit of Glasgwm descend west then south-west by the ridge fence to an intersection of fences (GR 831193). Descend left by the fence to the col beneath the slopes of Pen Waun-wen before following the normal descent route as above.

Other route options

The obvious options are the southern approaches from the A470 at Cwm Cerist using forestry tracks to the ridge between Pen Waun-wen and Glasgwm, but they're not strictly legal and you may be challenged. There is a legal route from Bwlch Oerddrws, higher on the A470, climbing first to Pen y Brynfforchog and then by the forest's edge to Glasgwm.

RIDGE ROUTES

Aran Fawddwy

Distance: 2¾ miles/4.4km
Height gain: 1150ft/350m
Time: 1¼ hours

From the summit cairn descend past Llyn Bach and by the fence down to the col before crossing Waun Camddwr. The ill-defined ridge becomes bouldery as height is gained. Near the top the route is met by the path from Drws Bach and together they follow the fence for most of the way to the trig point, which lies a short way to the east of the fence.

Pen y Brynfforchog

Distance: 1¾ miles/2.8km
Height gain: 245ft/75m
Time: ¾ hour

From the east summit cairn follow the fence to the right of Llyn y Fign on to the slightly higher but featureless western summit. The fence guides the route to a ladder stile by a fence intersection looking down on a large conifer plantation.

Follow a faint path around a rock-and-grass hollow to the northern edge of the forest, which should be traced to another fence intersection at the forest corner (GR 817184). From there you climb left (south-wards) on grassy slopes to Pen y Brynffor-chog's summit.

Pen Waun-wen

Distance: 1½ miles/2.3km
Height gain: 130ft/40m (690ft/210m descent)
Time: ¾ hour

Descend from the cairned east summit to the lake, where a ladder stile straddles the fence. Head south down rough grass slopes, with Craig Cywarch coming into view ahead. In the later stages you'll come close to the top edge of the crags (take care). Go over a ladder stile at the col and climb the easy grass slopes to Pen Waun-wen's summit.

Pen y Brynfforchog means summit of the forked hill, and presumably refers to the fork formed by the twin southern spurs above the valley of the Cerist. This grassy southern outpost of the main Aran ridge looks across the high pass of Bwlch Oerddrws to Cwm Cerist, the Dyfi Hills and outwards to Cardigan Bay. Although it's almost crag-free and overgrown with spruce trees in the east, it's still a fine peak with a narrow south-west spur which makes a splendid descent route into Cwm Cerist.

The peak is often the first visited on an itinerary of the main Aran ridge, and provides an early vantage point before moving on to higher places.

Opposite: Pen y Brynfforchog seen across Bwlch Oerddrws.
Below: The south ridge of Pen y Brynfforchog, looking towards Bwlch Oerddrws.

Route AH12
Bwlch Oerddrws
A steep route on grassy slopes and ridges
Start: Bwlch Oerddrws (GR: SH 802170)
Distance: 1½ miles/2.4km
Height gain: 1115ft/340m
Time: 1 hour

From the car park cross the road and go over the stile in the fence. It would be possible to make a bold course by the fence now on your right straight up the hillside, but a better bet is to follow sheep-trods angling left to reach the crest of the grassy spur Ochr y Bwlch.

Now follow the easy slopes of the crest, climbing to the right to a subsidiary summit (564m), where you'll see a grassy spur rising northwards to Pen y Brynfforchog. This is a delectable journey on easy grass with breathtaking views back to Cribin Fawr and its yawning cwm. Within a mile the journey is done: the summit of Pen y Brynfforchog widens the earlier views to include Cadair Idris and the Rhinogs.

Other route options
Tracks from Brithdir climb to access land to the west of the summit but the routes would be rough and often pathless.

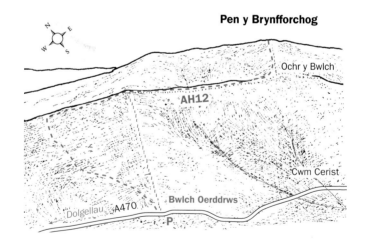

Pen y Brynfforchog

222

RIDGE ROUTE

Glasgwm

Distance: 1¾ miles/2.8km
Height gain: 540ft/165m
Time: ¾–1 hour

Descend northwards with the forest on your right, then turn right alongside the fence, which traces the northern edge of the plantation. A short way beyond Bwlch y Fign follow a faint path arcing left around a grass-and-rock hollow to reach a ladder stile by a fence intersection at a corner of the plantation att GR 827189.

Now follow the fence heading north-east up the barren Glasgwm ridge, first reaching the higher west summit, then passing to the left of the windswept waters of Llyn y Fign. Beyond this the path leads you to the cairn on the east summit.

Right: Cadair Idris from Pen y Brynfforchog.

PEN WAUN-WEN

Pen Waun-wen is the domed peak seen from the valley floor of Cwm Cywarch, where it is totally dominated by the great buttresses and rocks of Craig Cywarch. Although the mountain is largely grassy, crag does break free above the hollow of Cwm yr Ychen.

On the west side, above Cwm Cerist, its rocks and great waterfalls have suffered the indignity of being engulfed by conifers, and the bulldozed forestry road continues in huge zigzags across grassland, virtually to the summit.

Pen Waun-wen is barely higher than the pass between it and Glasgwm, but it is the highest point of the long grassy ridge declining to the cottages of Dinas Mawddwy. The ridge south-west of the summit becomes excitingly narrow, though still grassy as it descends to Bwlch yr Anges.

As part of a walk along this ridge it is a worthwhile objective, and as a viewpoint for the crags and mountainsides surrounding the verdant Cwm Cywarch it is certainly second to none. Luckily an old miners' track from Cywarch does form a spectacular highway to the top on this eastern side.

Note: on the OS Landranger map, this is named only as Y Gribin, which actually is the name of the ridge.

Left: Pen Waun-wen from Cwm Cywarch.

Route AH13
Cwm Cywarch

A stunning route among the crags of the cwm

Start: Cwm Cywarch (GR: SH 853187)
Distance: 2 miles/3.2km
Height gain: 1540ft/470m
Time: 1¼ hours

Turn right out of the car park and follow the road back to an open area of common land, Fawnog Fawr. Here a stony vehicle track angles right to ford a stream (this can be difficult after heavy rain) and continues past the cottage of Gesail and a ruin beyond it.

Note that the right of way marked on the map hasn't existed on the ground for a long time, and has been replaced in practice by the track you're on. (The right of way would have crossed the horrible field of rushes you see half-left and continued on a narrow spur between two streams that is now choked with head-high bracken.)

Continue with the track as it zigzags up Cwm Cywarch beneath spectacular rock-faces, which are softened by the greenery of the lower slopes and the fine rowan trees.

On reaching the top of the track and the col turn left and climb the easy grass slopes to Pen Waun-wen's summit.

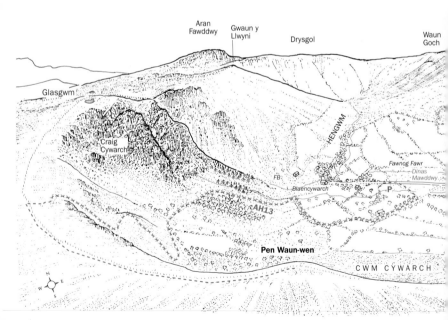

Other route options

Paths and tracks from the road in Cwm Cerist never quite make it into the access areas: one descending from the ridge even ends halfway down. Many people use the forest route, but it is not strictly legal and you could be turned back. In theory the track from the campsite at Dinas Mawddwy does reach access land at Pentre to the west, but in practice the slopes are rough and steep.

RIDGE ROUTES

Glasgwm

Distance: 1½ miles/2.3km
Height gain: 690ft/210m
Time: 1 hour

Descend the grass ridge north-westwards to the col, then go over the step stile near a fence intersection. Don't cross the adjacent ladder stile but follow the narrow path near the cliff edge. (In bad ice, snow or mist follow the fence until GR 837188, where it turns left, then head north to the summit.)

The main path climbs north to the summit lake, Llyn y Fign. Go over the stile in the fence to the right of the lake and continue north for the east summit cairn.

Foel Benddin

Distance: 1 mile/1.7km
Height gain: 330ft/100m
Time: ½ hour

From the domed summit, descend the grassy ridge of Y Gribin with crags plummeting down to Cywarch on the left. The ridge narrows as it drops to Bwlch yr Anges. A steady climb leads to Foel Benddin's flat grassy summit.

Left: Pen Waun-wen's west ridge.

This rather ungainly peak and its subsidiary summit Foel Rhudd are drained by three rivers: the Twrch, the Llaethnant and the Groes. Happily, this doesn't mean it's boggy, for the top and sides are largely grassy. The pale colours of its moorland grasses give the mountain its name, which means the white ridges.

The mountain throws out one rather nice ridge northwards between Cwm Croes and Cwm Twrch and one narrower connecting ridge leading to the peat hags and groughs of Lechwedd Du.

The summit is crowned by a modest cairn, where some of the stones are of gleaming white quartz. The views from here are dominated by the eastern cliffs of Aran Fawddwy and Aran Benllyn, but these views are slightly restricted by the peak in between – Foel Hafod-fynydd.

Opposite: Esgeiriau Gwynion seen across Cwm Croes.
Below: On the path from Cwm Croes up to Bwlch Sirddyn.

Route AH14

Cwm Croes and Bwlch Sirddyn

A route dominated in the early stages by
*   tarred country lanes*

Start: Car park at Llanuwchllyn
    (GR: SH 879298)

Distance: 5½ miles/8.8km

Height gain: 1900ft/580m

Time: 3½ hours

Once out of the car park, turn left along the B4403 road, across the bridge spanning the Afon Twrch and around the corner to the junction with the Bwlch y Groes mountain road. (You could use a short-cut path from the east side of the ridge to the mountain road at the cottage of Pen-rhiw Dwrch.) Either way, follow the mountain road to Talardd, where you turn right again into the pretty pastured valley of Cwm Croes.

Follow the lane to the last occupied farm, Nant-y-barcut, and go through the farmyard, beyond which a track continues south further into the valley. Leave this for a less obvious track on the left, which passes some ruined outbuildings before descending pastures to the uninhabited Cwm-ffynnon. After traversing some rushy ground beyond Cwm-ffynnon the path traces the lower edges of a field before maintaining direction on open hillside on the eastern flanks of Cwm Ddu.

Now very faint on the ground, the path heads towards the dark conical crag to the left of the cascade at the head of the valley. As it nears the crag the path becomes clearer and takes the route to a cross-fence at Bwlch Sirddyn. Here you leave the path and climb left by the fence, which leads to the little cairn on the summit.

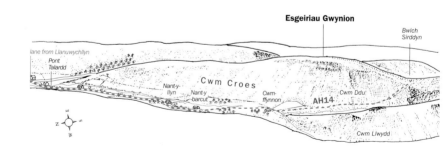

Route AH15
Bwlch y Groes and Llechwedd Du

A rough, damp, moorland ridge walk
Start: Bwlch y Groes (GR: SH 913233)
Distance: 2¼ miles/3.7km
Height gain: 560ft/170m
Time: 1½ hours

The route starts high (1787ft/545m) on the wild peatlands and tussocks of Bwlch y Groes, but this walk is no pushover. There's a fence all the way but those tussocks and the peat hags will be the theme of the journey.

A track from the back of the car park fades into these tussocks and you're left with a high-level moorland tramp, which is at its worst on Clipiau Duon. After turning north at a fence corner beyond Llechwedd Du the going eases. Any peat hags are now well-spaced islands with easy grass in between.

The ridge narrows, with Bwlch Sirddyn on your left and the valley of the Twrch on your right. Still following the fence, climb north-west on to the slopes, then the summit of Esgeiriau Gwynion.

Above: The peat hags of Llechwedd Ddu.

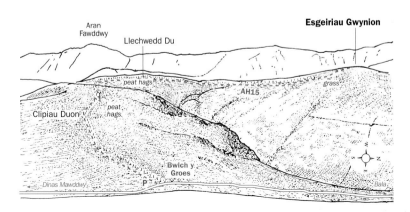

Route AH16
Blaen-pennant

A pleasant route until the last summit pull
Start: Blaen-pennant (GR: SH 905214)
Distance: 2½ miles/4km
Height gain: 2525ft/480m
Time: 1½ hours

Leave the road at Blaen-pennant on a rough stony track climbing above Llaethnant stream and beneath craggy hillslopes. The path is diverted from the track to avoid Blaen-pennant farm but rejoins soon afterwards and continues beneath the slopes of Lechwedd Du.

After a zigzag, the track leaves the Llaethnant valley and heads north up the valley of the Ceunant y Briddell. Now grassy, it climbs to the marshy pass of Bwlch Sirddyn, which overlooks the pastured valley of Cwm Croes. Here the track becomes a path and you leave it for a steep fence-side climb on rough grassy slopes to the right. This leads to the summit.

Other route options

I've seen many guidebooks list the route from Pont Talardd up the north ridge, but the route is not legal and you would need permission from the farmer on the north side.

RIDGE ROUTES

Moel y Cerrig Duon
Distance: 3½ miles/5.5km
Height gain: 460ft/140m
Time: 2 hours

Follow the fence descending east, then south-east, to the narrow saddle between the valleys of Ceunant y Briddell and the Twrch, before climbing south to the peat hags of Lechwedd Du. It's hard to believe it from here but this peak has some fine crags and screes tumbling into the upper Dyfi Valley.

The fence and the route now turn eastwards over the marshes of Clipiau Duon

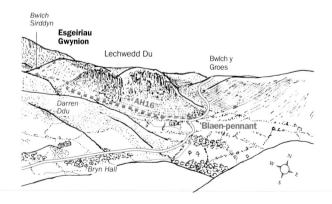

before heading north-eastwards to join a farm track leading to the car park at Bwlch y Groes. Across the road another fence leads over rough grassland eventually to reach the summit of Moel y Cerrig Duon.

Foel Hafod-fynydd

Distance: 1¼ miles/2km
Height gain: 590ft/180m
Time: ¾ hour

Descend the steep, grassy south-west spur, keeping the fence nearby to reach the pass, Bwlch Sirddyn. The grass slopes of Foel Hafod-fynydd soar to the sky and it's a tough pull to the summit. So it's better to zigzag up the pathless slopes of Gors Lwyd (on the left) to keep the gradient bearable rather than following the continuing fence. Once on the ridge turn right and follow the fence to the little cairn on the summit.

Below: The track between Blaen Pennant and Bwlch Sirddyn.

Overlooking the valleys of the Llaethant and Cwm Croes, Foel Hafod-fynydd is somewhat in the shadow of its higher western neighbour Aran Fawddwy. It's a grassy hill with only a smattering of crags, but it's a shapely hill with a fine narrow northern spur, Braich-yr-hwch, which declines into Cwm Croes and separates two romantic little corries, Cwm Llwydd and Cwm Ddu. The high slopes above the latter are enhanced by the rocks of Craig Cwm-du.

Perhaps Foel Hafod-fynydd's finest feature is its views, for the unyielding nearby crags, cliffs and gullies of Aran Fawddwy and Aran Benllyn soar in tremendous fashion to the skyline, decorated by the beautifully sited tarn Creiglyn Dyfi, the source of the great Afon Dyfi, which flows out to Cardigan Bay.

Route AH17

Cwm Croes and Braich-yr-hwch

A splendid climb with spectacular views of the big Aran's crags

Start: Car park at Llanuwchllyn (GR: SH 880298)

Distance: 5½ miles/8.8km

Height gain: 1900ft/580m

Time: 3½ hours

Once out of the car park, turn left along the road, across the bridge spanning the Afon Twrch and around the corner to the junction with the Bwlch y Groes mountain road. You could also use a short-cut path from the east side of the ridge to the mountain road at the cottage of Pen-rhiw Dwrch. Whichever one you choose, follow the mountain road to Talardd, where you turn right again into the pretty pastured valley of Cwm Croes. Follow the lane to the last occupied farm, Nant-y-barcut, and go through the farmyard, beyond

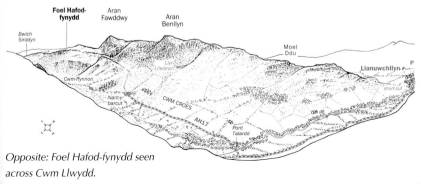

Opposite: Foel Hafod-fynydd seen across Cwm Llwydd.

which a track continues south further into the valley. Leave this for a less obvious track on the left, which passes some ruined outbuildings before descending pastures to the uninhabited Cwm-ffynnon.

Beyond the old farm follow a track over the bridge spanning the infant Afon Groes, then take the track fording the stream on the right. Leave the track to head for the base of Braich-yr-hwch, a superb grassy spur taking you up to the mountains.

Climb to the crest of this narrow spur, which can now be followed to a subsidiary summit. Now climb by the fence all the way to the ridge linking Foel Hafod-fynydd with the main Aran ridge. Here the fence makes an acute angle left to climb south-east to the little cairn on the summit of Foel Hafod-fynydd.

Descent

The descent is fairly straightforward. Follow the fence WNW to where it doubles back right, leading down the grassy northern spur. Beyond a subsidiary summit, the ridge narrows and soon the fence ceases to be of any use as it descends half-left into Cwm Llwydd.

On reaching the bottom of the spur descend north-east to the grass track fording Cwm Ddu's stream before coming to the ruins of Cwm-ffynnon farm. From here a faint track heads north to the right of a conifer copse to meet a lane just short of Nant-y-bar-cut farm. Turn right along this, and pass through the farmyard out on to the Cwm Croes road. Continue along this to Pont Talardd where you turn left for Llanuwchllyn.

Above: Descending Braich-yr-hwch on Foel Hafod-fynydd.
Opposite: On the summit of Foel Hafod-fynydd looking across Creiglyn Dyfi to Aran Fawddwy.

RIDGE ROUTES

Esgeiriau Gwynion
Distance: 1¼ miles/2km
Height gain: 560ft/170m
Time: ¾ hour

From the little summit cairn follow the fence ESE across the tufty grass ridge, but beyond a fence intersection make your way downhill to the north to the saddle of land at Bwlch Sirddyn. Now Esgeiriau Gwynion stands before you with its equally steep grass slopes. It's a tough climb but it's soon done as the slopes ease and a spur of sorts develops, leading to the little cairn of white stones that marks the summit.

Aran Fawddwy
Distance: 1¼ miles/2.8km
Height gain: 1115ft/340m
Time: 1 hour

This fine route finds one of the few weaknesses in the craggy eastern flanks of the Aran. The views are dominated by the cliffs and Creiglyn Dyfi, a splendidly sited tarn at their foot.

Beginning on the grassy summit of Foel Hafod-fynydd, descend westwards, rounding the rim of Cwm Llwyd and the north-east shores of Creiglyn Dyfi. Now a steep grassy spur takes the route between the cliffs on to the main ridge. Turn left and follow the path on the far side of the fence to the trig point on Aran Fawddwy's summit.

This verdant and velvety, steep-sided mountain and its sister peak Pen yr Allt Isaf dominate the eastern side of Cwm Cywarch, and contrast beautifully with the stark crags on the far valley side.

Pen yr Allt Uchaf separates the deep grassy chasms of Hengwm and Cwm Terwyn and, unlike its sister peak, isn't yet troubled by unsympathetic forestry plantations. The summit, like the sides, is grassy, with a ridge fence running along its length. It's worth continuing to the end summit (616m spot height) to maximise those views.

Many walkers have set foot on this mountain, but are oblivious to its charms, for once they reach the head of Hengwm they turn with the footpath in the other direction towards Drysgol and Aran Fawddwy.

Opposite: Pen yr Allt Uchaf seen across Blaen Cywarch.
Below: Pen yr Allt Uchaf from Blaen Cywarch, showing the Route AH18 track from the valley floor to the foot of the mountain.

Route AH18
Cwm Cywarch and Hengwm

A classic Aran route

Start: Cwm Cywarch (GR: SH 853187)
Distance: 3 miles/4.7km
Height gain: 1805ft/505m
Time: 2 hours

Turn left out of the car park for a few paces before turning right on a signed footpath, which crosses a footbridge over the Afon Cywarch before climbing on a rough track by trees and hedges. Turn left along the farm track raking across the hillslopes into Hengwm, a beautiful deep hollow hemmed in on all sides by verdant but steep-sided mountains.

On reaching a marshy col at the head of the cwm, turn right, climbing SSE on grassy slopes up to Waun Goch. Now head south-west along the broad ridge, with conifers below and to the left. The ridge narrows beyond a subsidiary summit and cross-fence and the route continues easily to Pen yr Allt Uchaf.

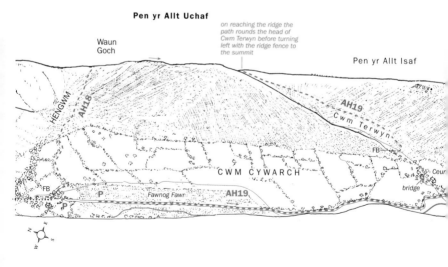

Pen yr Allt Uchaf

Waun Goch

on reaching the ridge the path rounds the head of Cwm Terwyn before turning left with the ridge fence to the summit

Pen yr Allt Isaf

HENGWM

AH18

AH19

Cwm Terwyn

FB

CWM CYWARCH

Ceur

bridge

FB

P

Fawnog Fawr

AH19

P

Opposite: Climbing Cwm Terwyn to Pen yr Allt Uchaf.

Route AH19
Cwm Cywarch and Cwm Terwyn
An old, seldom-used highway to the tops
Start: Fawnog Fawr common, Cwm Cywarch
   (GR: SH 854185)
Distance: 3¼ miles/5.3km
Height gain: 1705ft/520m
Time: 2 hours

From the car park by the information board at the end of the common, walk back down the road past the old chapel. The right of way (not signed at present) begins beyond the cottage of Terwyn on a farm track that heads north-east with a stream, Nant Terwyn, to the left.

Just past a cottage the track crosses a bridge over the stream and comes to some tree-shaded outbuildings, where you'll see a ladder stile on the left. Once over this, climb east with the stream below on your right, and go over the next ladder stile. A damp path maintains direction until an arrow pointing right directs the route down to a wooden bridge spanning the Nant Terwyn. Across this the path continues to a rushy track, which will rake up to the head of the valley.

Turn left up this ancient track and follow it over several side streams (soggy crossings at times). You come to the head of the valley beneath a rounded grassy knoll. Now turn left along a broad grassy ridge with forestry over to your right. Beyond a corner of the forest you'll encounter a fence, which you'll follow around the cwm. It will eventually lead all the way to the summit.

Descent

Descend the grassy ridge north-eastwards, then follow the ridge fence around the head of Cwm Terwyn. Where the fence veers a little left leave it and head south-east for the rounded knoll by a sharp forest corner. Watch out for a faint rushy groove on the right beneath the knoll. This is the start of the old track down Cwm Terwyn – the line can quite clearly be seen ahead as it's highlighted by rushes.

Near the bottom of the cwm waymarker arrows direct you off the track and down to a wooden bridge over Nant Terwyn, then left above the far banks of the stream. Over two ladder stiles the route comes to some farm outbuildings shaded by trees. Turn left on a track crossing a stone bridge taking you back over the stream, past the farmhouse and out to the Cywarch road. From here you turn right to head back to Fawnog Fawr common.

Other route options

You could make an approach from Llany-mawddwy up Cwm Dyniewyd and past its waterfalls. The edge of the forest beyond would lead to Waun Goch and onwards to the summit. See Route AH5.

RIDGE ROUTES

Aran Fawddwy

Distance: 2¾ miles/4.5km
Height gain: 1180ft/360m
Time: 1¾–2 hours

After descending the grassy ridge north-eastwards, go over the stile in the cross-fence to continue over Waun Goch where you descend north to the col at the head of Hengwm. Here you're joined by the well-used track from Cwm Cywarch and you now climb with it, mostly alongside a ridge fence to the summit of Drysgol.

Now the view northwards becomes spectacular, with the craggy dome and cliffs of Aran Fawddwy soaring from the waters of Creiglyn Dyfi, one of the best-situated tarns in southern Snowdonia. The ridge now becomes narrow and craggier, climbing on to Drws Bach, where you pass a memorial cairn before climbing rocky slopes on to Aran Fawddwy's main ridge. From here head north to the trig point.

Pen yr Allt Isaf

Distance: 1¾ miles/2.8km
Height gain: 165ft/50m
Time: 1 hour

Descend the grassy ridge north-eastwards, then follow the ridge fence around the head of Cwm Terwyn. Where the fence veers a little left leave it and head south-east for the rounded knoll by an acute corner. Pass to the right of a grassy knoll (585m spot height) to reach another forest corner. Now head south, keeping the plantation's edge and the ridge fence to the left. The true summit lies just beyond an intersection of fences.

Opposite: Pen yr Allt Uchaf from the south in Cwm Cywarch.

Not often visited because it doesn't make the magic 2000-foot mark, Pen yr Allt Isaf is none the worse for that. It's the slightly smaller twin of Pen yr Allt Uchaf, with the same steep grassy sides and slightly tussocky grass summit ridge. Forestry plantations have crept on to its eastern slopes from Cwm Isaf.

Routes up are enhanced by the distinctively shaped rocky knoll of Tarren Fawr and the twisting ravine of Y Ceunant, which lies beneath that peak. The little conical knoll of Tarren Fach is clad on its northern flanks with delightful broadleaved woods overlooking the rushing stream of Nant yr Aber.

Route AH20
Aber Cywarch and Bryn Sion

A splendid route to a fine viewpoint

Start: Aber Cywarch, very limited parking near phone box (GR: SH 868158)

Distance: 2¼ miles/3.5km

Height gain: 1510ft/460m

Time: 1½–2 hours

Note: this is a permissive route based on a Tir Gofal agreement. Please be considerate.

From the telephone box in the hamlet of Aber Cywarch turn left up the Cwm Cywarch road. On the approach to Bryn Sion you'll notice the low but distinctive knoll of Tarren Fawr,

Opposite: Tarren Fawr and the gorge of Y Ceunant.
Below: On the summit of Pen yr Allt Isaf with Craig Cywarch in the hazy distance.

then a farm track raking right past the farm of Yr-aber (a signed Tir Gofal track).

Beyond the farm buildings the track bends right beneath copses of larch before entering the tightly enclosed valley of Nant yr Aber. It's very pretty here, with the conical Tarren Fach's slopes cloaked with deciduous woodland and a lively stream tumbling down the meadows to the valley below.

The track, now grassy but firm, and the valley bend to the left beneath Tarren Fawr and embark upon a steady climb up grassy slopes, almost to the summit of Tarren Fawr. Here you look down the dark heather-and-crag ravine of Y Ceunant with the great crags of Cywarch forming a splendid backdrop.

The track continues its climb towards Bwlch Sycan, where you can see a feathered horizon of spruce trees. The track turns left just short of the trees but turns back to round the corner of the plantation. The track soon fades and a Tir Gofal sign directs you left.

Carry on a few paces here and it will save you walking over tussocks, for a faint track bends left and takes you to the ridge fence, where you're confronted by a choice of three little knolls, each vying for recognition as the summit. The one that is actually the highest is the nearest to the fence intersection.

Descent

From the summit head east on a faint path towards the spruce forest then turn right on a track following the plantation edge. The prominent track turns left to Bwlch Sychan before descending a grassy ridge to Tarren

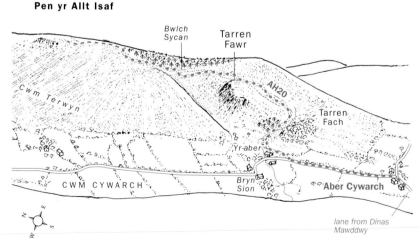

Pen yr Allt Isaf

Bwlch Sycan

Tarren Fawr

Cwm Terwyn

AH20

Tarren Fach

Yr-aber

CWM CYWARCH

Bryn Sion

Aber Cywarch

lane from Dinas Mawddwy

Fawr, from where it winds down to the farm buildings of Yr-aber. Turn left along the lane back to Aber Cywarch.

Other route options

As with Pen yr Allt Uchaf, you could make an approach from Llanymawddwy up Cwm Dyniewyd and past its waterfalls. The east and north edges of the forest beyond would by-pass Waun Goch to reach the head of Cwm Terwyn. By turning left to round the cwm you re-join the forest's edge and head southwards for the summit.

Below: The fine track to Pen yr Allt Isaf from Bryn Sion.

RIDGE ROUTE

Pen yr Allt Uchaf

Distance: 1¼ miles/2.8km
Height gain: 360ft/110m
Time: 1 hour

From the summit, Pen yr Allt Uchaf is on your left across the deep grassy chasm of Cwm Terwyn. Follow the ridge fence north-east to the conifers, then follow the plantation's edge. Beyond the forest corner turn left along a broad grassy ridge. When you encounter the fence again at another forest corner, follow it around the cwm. The fence will eventually lead all the way to Pen yr Allt Uchaf's summit.

MOEL Y CERRIG DUON

This rather dull 2000-foot summit lies just above Bwlch y Groes, a high pass straddled by the Llanuwchllyn to Dinas Mawddwy mountain road, not far from its junction with the Lake Vyrnwy road. Drained by the Afon Eiddew and Afon Eunant, which feed into Lake Vyrnwy, the mountain's summit is on the very edge of Snowdonia, with its eastern slopes outside the national park.

It's a grassy domed hill topped by a small cairn with a pole in the middle, and lies at the end of a very rough ill-defined ridge linking the Aran mountains with those of the Hirnant.

Moel y Cerrig Duon does have a few craggy outcrops above the Vyrnwy road and some squat cliffs, Craig yr Ogof (crag of the cave), in the west. It also has a partial view of Lake Vyrnwy, but all this is not enough for sustained interest.

Opposite: Moel y Cerrig Duon from Foel y Geifr.
Below: The summit of Moel y Cerrig Duon with Lake Vyrnwy in the distance.

Route AH21
Lake Vyrnwy and Pistyll Rhyd-y-meinciau

Good for distant views, avoiding the worst of the heather and tussocks

Start: Rhiwargor car park, Lake Vyrnwy
(GR: SH 964241)

Distance: 3 miles/4.8km

Height gain: 1230ft/375m

Time: 1¾ hours

The best option and a more satisfying ascent of Moel y Cerrig Duon for the purist begins at the northern end of Lake Vyrnwy, where there's a waymarked trail to the waterfalls of Pistyll Rhyd-y-meinciau.

The path from the back of the car park heads across fields on the south side of the Afon Eiddew with the crags of Allt y Gribin on one side and the spruce-clad slopes of Bwlan on the other. Ignore both footbridges across the river for they're part of a circular walk taking you back to the car park.

The falls are quite magnificent with great torrents of foaming white water crashing down in a series of big craggy steps. Birch trees soften the scene nicely as do the tea-coloured pools below the torrents.

A path now climbs the south banks high above the falls and continues alongside the river through the upper moorland valley of

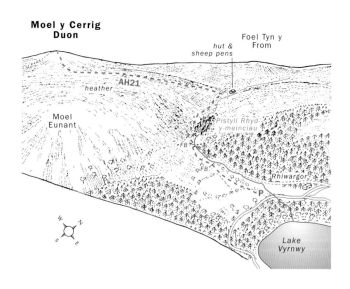

Opposite: The waterfalls of Pistyll Rhyd-y-meinciau near the head of Lake Vyrnwy.

the Eiddew. The river takes some time to calm down and still flows in lively cataracts a mile or so beyond the main falls. Eventually it does, and the scene becomes one of tussocks and heather with anonymous rounded moors in all directions. By this time the path has given up and you find yourself searching for the least tussocky terrain. As usual in these situations you'll end up following the tracks of our little woolly friends.

Eventually you reach the confluence of the Eiddew Fawr and Eiddew Fach, where there's a remote ruined hut with a brick chimney and extensive sheep pens next door. Here you leave the valley and strike up south-westwards across the moors. There's a grassy channel to help. The rounded outlines of Moel y Cerrig Duon are dominant on the shoulder of the slopes you're climbing.

Again there are no paths but management of the heather means that there are strips of mown vegetation to help you climb to the ridge top. Once on top the way is clear, with your destination straight ahead. The going isn't too bad across the heather, and indeed improves on the final pull on grass to the summit fence.

Other route options
The obvious one is the short ridge walk from the top of the Bwlch y Groes road. You just follow the fence on grass all the way to the summit. It's short, painless and you'll get a glimpse of Lake Vyrnwy without much effort.

RIDGE ROUTES

Esgeiriau Gwynion

Distance: 3½ miles/5.5km
Height gain: 625ft/190m
Time: 2 hours

The ridge fence/wall acts as a guide all the way south-west to the high lane at Bwlch y Groes. Go across the car park and follow the vehicle track south-west along a peaty ridge. Again there's a fence all the way but the tussocks and the peat will be the theme of the journey.

The track fades into these tussocks and you're left with a high-level moorland tramp, which is at its worst on Clipiau Duon. After turning north beyond the summit of Llechwedd Du the ridge narrows, with Bwlch Sirddyn on your left and the valley of the Twrch on your right. Still following the fence, climb north-west beyond this on to the slopes, then the summit, of Esgair Gwynion.

Opposite: Descending Moel y Cerrig Duon's ridge towards Bwlch y Groes.

Foel y Geifr

Distance: 3 miles/4.8km
Height gain: 590ft/180m
Time: 2 hours

To call this a ridge route is stretching a point, but for completeness I have to include a walk that is arduous and pointless. It is also very difficult to navigate in mist, as the fence straddling Moel y Cerrig Duon's summit ceases to be a ridge fence and instead undulates over spurs and across the valleys of the Eiddew and Nadroedd.

The way starts as it means to go on, over trackless rough heather and peat. Head NNW, rounding the head of the Eiddew valley, whose trickling stream eventually guides the route to Foel Tyn-y-from, a horribly marshy hill. After crossing the fence on this summit descend NNE across more heather before climbing on rough moor grass to Cefn Coch, where the valley of Nant Nadroedd leads your eyes past a spread of spruce trees to the headwaters of Lake Vyrnwy.

The way forward now is north-east along a narrowing moorland ridge between Nant Nadroedd and Nant yr Eira. This leads to Mynydd Carnedd Hywel, where heather takes over again and the vast conifer plantations of Penllyn Forest come into view. A fence comes in from the left and guides the route almost to Foel y Geifr's summit. Cross the fence at an intersection to reach your destination.

Foel y Geifr, the bare hill of the goat, is the highest summit on a long spur declining to Cwm Hirnant. It's the northern outlier of an ill-defined ridge that ends at Moel y Cerrig Duon, overlooking the high pass of Bwlch y Groes between Llanuwchllyn and Dinas Mawddwy.

Other than that it's over 2,000 feet high, I cannot think of any reason to walk on Foel y Geifr. Logical legal routes are impossible to find. If you must do it, then do it the quickest way, which is from the top of the Bala to Lake Vyrnwy road.

The view from its grassy summit with a scattering of quartz rocks might just about justify such a short journey. In the direction of the Aran ridge the distant views are reasonably good, although slightly obscured by Esgeiriau Gwynion and Foel Hafod-fynydd.

Opposite: Climbing from the top of the Cwm Hirnant road to Foel y Geifr.
Below: The summit of Foel y Geifr.

Route AH22

Cwm Hirnant

Good for distant views and avoiding the worst of the heather and tussocks

Start: The top of Cwm Hirnant road
(GR: SH 946274)

Distance: ¾ mile/1.3km

Height gain: 460ft/140m

Time: ½ hour

This is a short, dull journey across rough marshy grassland then heather to reach the oasis of grass and stones forming the summit of Foel y Geifr. From the back of the car park there's a faint vehicle track leading to a low fence.

Once across this there's a large expanse of marsh and heather to cross, but beyond this grassy channels lead through the heather heading for the summit cairn, which you can see on the left end of the escarpment. Keeping a fence well to the left, follow the grass as it leads upwards towards the ridge. You'll soon join a narrow path climbing to the trig point.

Other route options

You could begin at the cattle grid in Cwm Hirnant (GR 950290), cross the stream and fence and climb north-west, then north along the top edges of the field on the right to reach the edge of the forest (GR 950256). An adjoining fence would then lead the route up steep slopes on to Foel Goch. Now a rough ridge route leads SSW over heather, passing the summit of Trum y Gwrgedd before coming to Foel y Geifr.

Foel y Geifr

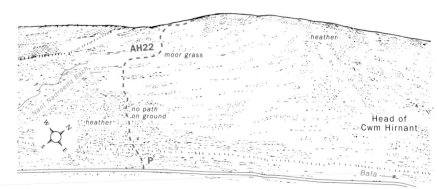

RIDGE ROUTES

Moel y Cerrig Duon
Distance: 3 miles/4.8km
Height gain: 590ft/180m
Time: 2 hours

This is a rough, ill-defined and utterly point-less exercise in how much pain you can put your body through and how much tedium you can inflict on your mind. There are no paths so the key to the route is finding the easiest terrain, which is usually the grassy or straw-coloured bits rather than the thick heather or the peat bog.

Make your way to the fence to the south-west and follow it around the head of the cwm of Nant Nadroedd Fawr. The terrain is one of tussocks, heather and bog as you climb to the intermediate summit Cefn Coch.

The theme continues on a SSW course across a confusing moorland complex of ridges and spurs, over the ghastly Foel Tyn-y-from, where you cross a fence and head south-west then south to avoid a feeder stream of Nant Eiddew Fawr. Keep slightly to the east side of the ridge at Pen y Cefn before descending to a broad col beneath Moel y Cerrig Duon. Climb south-east to reach the grassy summit, topped with a pole and a cairn.

Cyrniau Nod
Distance: 4½ miles/ 7.2km
Height gain: 1015ft/310m
Time: 2½ hours

Descend on a narrow path southwards at first. Where the path gives up veer left, keeping to grassy rides away from the heather and well away from the fence and stream on your right. You'll probably be able to make out faint vehicle tracks from time to time and these lead towards the car parking area at the top of the Bala to Lake Vyrnwy road.

Eventually the grass gives out and you need to cross a damp area of heather. After straddling the low fence continue across more heather, then tussocky grass to the car park.

On the opposite side of the road you'll see a flinty track leading easily over the rough heather hills of the Hirnant with the vast conifer plantations of the Penllyn Forest on its left. Between Foel Cedig and Y Groes Fagl, and just before the track makes a sharp left turn to descend to the forest, watch out for a narrow path on the right (GR 988285).

This leads to a fence, then follows it to the right to reach an intersection of fences. Here step over the one on your left and head south on a narrow path through heather keeping the newly met fence to the right. Cyrniau Nod's summit is marked by a pole sticking out from a small cairn.

Cyrniau Nod is the highest peak of a high heathery ridge overlooking the Penllyn Forest and Bala's lake. It has been described by Alan Dawson in his book *Relative Hills* as a candidate for the most boring hill in Wales. Well, I know where he's coming from, for this is a heathery lump of a hill, with some approaches so tough that they make climbing Snowdon seem like a Sunday-school outing.

However, Cyrniau Nod has compensations, albeit intrinsic ones. It's remote and, apart from the fence and poled summit cairn, it's devilishly wild. Anything that gives as much trouble as the approach from beautiful Pennant Melangell has to be appreciated for the achievement that it is.

In August and September when the heather is in full bloom, there's a luscious colour about the place, not to mention the sweet aromas. On a clear day you can see as far as the hills of Radnor and the Brecon Beacons.

For those who just want to tick it off their lists, there's even an easy way, for a stony track leads from the top of the Bala to Lake Vyrnwy road and comes within a very short distance of the summit.

Route AH23
Cwm Hirnant

The route is about as easy as it gets on the Hirnant range

Start: Bwlch yr Hwch, Cwm Hirnant (GR: SH 952300)

Distance: 4½ miles/7.2km

Height gain: 1510ft/460m

Time: 2–2½ hours

From its junction with the Cwm Hirnant lane at Bwlch yr Hwch, follow the farm track from the left-hand side of the road. Ahead are the trees of Penllyn Forest. Take the right fork, which descends to the flat-topped stone hut at the valley bottom. The track climbs the hillside to the right of the hut and comes to a gate at the entrance to velvety green pastures.

Through the gate, climb steeply southwards and go through the gateway into the next field. Now angle right to follow the fence to the top gate. Beyond this a stony track climbs the heather slopes of Pen y Cerrig Duon to join and follow in an easterly direction the bulldozed stony track that winds among the many Hirnant tops. The top edge of Penllyn's vast coniferous trees is always dominant in a view which encompasses the twin peaks of Arenig Fawr, and the rugged rocky cwms of the Aran range.

Opposite: Cyrniau Nod seen across Cwm Pennant.

Above: On the summit of Cyrniau Nod looking south to Cwm Pennant.

If you have a mind to, you can detour right to visit first Pen y Cerrig Duon, then Pen y Boncyn Trefeilw, but they're just bumps on the landscape – the latter has its modest summit pile of stones set in farmland.

The track descends alongside the lower edge of more farm pastures before climbing again to the heather slopes of Foel Cedig. As it reaches its high point and just before the sharp left-hand bend a small cairn (hopefully still intact) marks the start of a narrow path on the right.

This cuts across low heather before turning right alongside a fence. Cross the low fence at an intersection before heading south by the new fence to the pole and pile of stones marking Cyrniau Nod's summit.

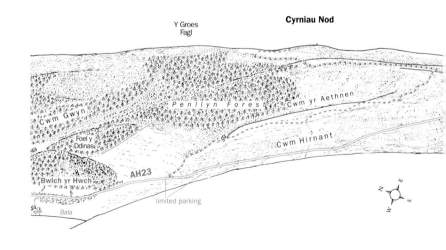

Route AH24

Pennant Melangell and Pistyll Blaen-y-cwm

A beautiful start, but a punishingly rough moorland finish

Start: Pennant Melangell car park
(GR: SJ 024265)

Distance: 3½ miles/6km

Height gain: 1640ft/500m

Time: 2½ hours

Pennant Melangell is an idyllic, peaceful place, green with field, hedgerow and woodland surrounding the sixteenth-century church and a handful of whitewashed and stone-built cottages. Your eyes rise up to the hills where crag, more woodland and spout-like waterfalls at the head of the valley add more beauty than anyone has the right to expect.

If you can bear to leave this place turn right out of the car park and follow the lane to the bridleway signposted to the waterfalls. Although the path is unclear on the ground, the sign shows the direction across a field to the first gate, where the route climbs slightly left to the next one. Additional waymarker posts highlight the route to another gate. Here a bridleway sign shows a climb to the right, but our route turns left on a grass path up the hillside towards the head of the valley.

Gorse and newly planted (in 2009) broadleaved trees line the narrowing path as it draws nearer and nearer to the falls. The path fords two streams and becomes much harder to trace. Once over the second stream do not be drawn on to a track on the left, which ends in impenetrable gorse, but instead climb slightly right before passing a tiny cairn.

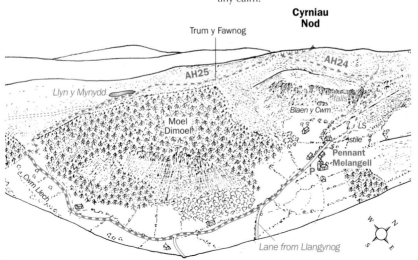

261

After passing a large crag the route descends towards the infant Tanat stream by a couple of rowan trees. Now any trace of a path ends. The helpful-looking track shown on current OS maps hereabouts doesn't exist on the ground and neither does that foot-bridge. In short sections you may be able to pick it out, either as a heather-and-rush filled hollow or as a tussocky grass channel through the heather. It's further obscured by patches of brashed or burned heather. So a decision has to be made.

Do you look for it – you'll need to keep referring to your Garmin, Satmap or Road Angel – or do you bite the bullet and head straight up the hillslopes for Cyrniau Nod?

Either way it's going to be tough, for the heather is thick, the ground very uneven for landing or lift-off of the feet, and the green patches promising better things are equally rough with horrid tussocks of moss.

I would go for the former option, following the traces of track where you can find them, because this way it's slightly shorter to the ridge, with less ascent, and has brief periods where the walking isn't torture on the limbs. Basically, from the Tanat stream above the waterfalls you head south-west towards Nant Llwyngwrgi, crossing it close to a confluence with a side stream.

Climb generally south-westwards to the ridge fence on Llanerch Wen. If you've been

Opposite: The falls at the head of Cwm Pennant.
Below: The crossing point of the infant Tanat.

accurate in your navigation there will be a step stile in the ridge, and the hollow you were in will continue on the other side.

Now the real hard work is over. Follow a faint path on the east side of the fence as it undulates through a terrain of heather, peat and mosses to the pile of stones and the pole marking the summit of Cyrniau Nod.

Below: Llyn y Mynydd, a stark mountain reservoir sited beneath Cyrniau Nod's south ridge.

Route AH25

Pennant Melangell and Llyn y Mynydd

A pleasing route through pasture, forest and finally on a ridge

Start: Pennant Melangell car park (GR: SJ 024265)

Distance: 5¼ miles/8.4km

Height gain: 1740ft/530m

Time: 2½ hours

Turn left out of the car park and continue back down the beautiful valley, taking two right forks beneath the rugged craggy slopes of Moel Dimoel into Cwm Llech. After passing the cottages and farmhouse at Pwlliago, the tarmac ends and a stony track continues up the now heavily afforested valley. The track soon enters the relative darkness of the forest.

Take the right fork track, which soon climbs with one zigzag out of the forest into a wilder cwm. By now you may have noticed the abundance of game birds, which are bred in these parts. As the path closes in on the Llyn y Mynydd reservoir there is a confusion of forest roads and farm tracks. Keep straight ahead to the right-hand end of the dam, before continuing on a grass track that rakes halfway up the slopes of Trum y Fawnog.

Sheepwalks continue on grass to the junction of fences at the ridge-top. Go over the simple stile here and follow the ridge fence, now on your left, over Llanerch Wen to the summit of Cyrniau Nod, easily recognisable with its pole and cairn.

Other route options

There is a long route from the shores of Lake Vyrnwy using the forestry tracks along the valley of the Afon Cedig. Beyond Hafoty Cedig, a narrow path follows the infant stream before climbing to the ridge at Llanerch Wen, where it's a fairly gentle climb to Cyrniau Nod's summit.

RIDGE ROUTES

Foel y Geifr

Distance: 4½ miles/7.2km
Height gain: 850ft/265m
Time: 2½ hours

Follow the ridge fence northwards to an intersection of fences and cross the one ahead.

Now turn right to follow a narrow path on the left side of the fence. The path veers left after a short way and leads to the stony track. Turn left along this and follow it all the way to the road at the head of Cwm Hirnant. Foel y Geifr now lies straight ahead beyond a car parking area.

From the back of the car park there's a faint vehicle track leading to a low fence. Once across this there's a large expanse of marsh and heather to cross, but beyond this grassy channels lead through the heather heading for the summit cairn, which you can see on the left end of the escarpment. Keeping a fence well to the left, follow the grass as it leads upwards towards the ridge. You'll soon join a narrow path climbing to the trig point.

Y Groes Fagl

Distance: ¾ mile/1.3km
Height gain: 870ft/30m
Time: ½ hour

Follow the ridge fence northwards to an intersection of fences. Now cross the fence ahead and turn right to follow a narrow path on the left side of the fence. The path veers left after a short way and leads to a stony track. This heads north at first but then swings left. Just beyond this bend a narrow path heads north to the pole on Y Groes Fagl's summit.

Y GROES FAGL

Y Groes Fagl, which lies in the centre of the Hirnant ridge, is a featureless mound, defended by peat hags, marshy mosses and thick heather. Its only saving graces are that it is over 2000 feet high, which makes it interesting to peak-baggers, and it has a stony forestry track passing close enough to its summit to make things easy.

The summit itself is grassy and capped by a wooden pole, not the cross you might expect from the name, which it has been suggested means snare's cross. Views are dominated by the main Berwyn ridge, which lies over the shoulder of the heathery Foel Cwm Sian-llwyd, and by Llyn Tegid (Bala Lake) which stretches beyond the Penllyn Forest to the Arenig horizon.

Opposite: Y Groes Fagl from the west.
Below: A storm brews over the summit of Y Groes Fagl.

Route AH26
Aber Hirnant and the Penllyn Forest

A long but easy climb on forest roads

Start: Roadside parking ½ mile/800m south
    of Aber Hirnant (GR: SH 957320)

Distance: 3¾ miles/ 6.1km

Height gain: 1475ft/450m

Time: 2 hours

From the roadside parking spot, head south along the Cwm Hirnant road until you reach the forestry track preceding Foel-y-ddinas farm (GR 953312). The stony road climbs steadily through the spruce and larch trees of Cwm Gwyn. Take the left fork to stay north of the pastures of Ystrad-y-groes and ignore all tracks and roads that descend right.

The required track keeps the Nant Ystrad-y-groes (stream) and its side-stream, Nant y Groes-fagl, to the right (south-west). Eventually it leaves the forest for the heather and grass ridge to the west of Y Groes Fagl. Just before a sharp right-hand bend leave the track for a narrow path on the left, which climbs north to the nearby summit pole.

Above: The little path from the forestry track to the summit of Y Groes Fagl.

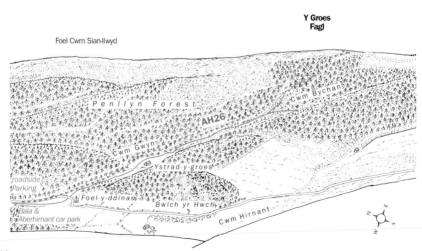

Y Groes
Fagl

Foel Cwm Sian-llwyd

Penllyn Forest

AH26

Cwm Bychan

Cwm Gwyn

Ystrad-y-groes

roadside Parking

Foel-y-ddinas

Bwlch yr Hwch

Bala & Aberhirnant car park

Cwm Hirnant

Route AH27

Milltir Gerrig and Hafod Hir

*A wild moorland route which starts high but
     ends rough*

Start: Car park Milltir Gerrig on B4391
     (GR: SJ 017305)

Distance: 3 miles/5km

Height gain: 755ft/230m

Time: 1½ hours

Descend SSE along the road in the direction
of Llangynog. After about 500 yards/m take
the track on the right leading around the head
of Cwm Rhiwarth. This is eventually joined
by a track climbing up from the valley. It is
well worth detouring for a short way down
this track to get a view of the waterfalls,
which otherwise would be missed.

Once you are back on the main track,
follow it over a ford by some spruce trees.

Beyond this the track becomes less prominent but follow a fainter path towards a fence
on the left. This course leads to a footbridge
over a stream.

Beyond the crossing a narrow path through
grass and rushes climbs the hillside to
the south. Ignore the several vehicle tracks
except where they join your path. The route
comes close to the hollow of Nant Caich
before reaching a gate in the ridge fence. Go
through the gate and turn right to follow the
fence across a rough moor of tussocky grass
and heather and over the summit of Bryn
Ysbio.

The terrain gets tougher as height is gained
and soon becomes a trudge across thick
heather and peat hags. Cross the fence that
traverses the high shoulder of Y Groes Fagl
before climbing just south of west to the pole
on its summit.

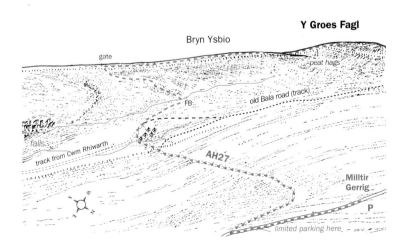

269

Descent

The key to the descent is to find the fence intersection on Y Groes Fagl's east side (GR 993292). By heading due east you'll come across it, with any final adjustments to be made when it comes into view across the heather and peat hags.

The fence ahead leads for just short of 2 miles/3.2km to the gate by another fence intersection (at GR 016286). Descend left along a clear path that soon runs parallel to Nant Caich. Ignore the wheel-tracks where they divert from the path, and maintain direction north as the path descends more steeply through rushy terrain to cross a footbridge.

Over a stile head north-east around the head of Cwm Rhiwarth towards a copse of conifers, where you join a prominent track and ford Nant Llwyn-gwern. Ignoring the right-forking Cwm Rhiwarth track, continue on the main track around the head of the cwm. This comes to the B4391. Turn left for the car park at Milltir Gerrig.

Below: The church at Pennant Melangell at the start of Route AH28.

Route AH28
Pennant Melangell

Contrasting scenes of a beautiful verdant valley and stark wild moorland

Start: Pennant Melangell car park (GR: SJ 024265)
Distance: 3½ miles /5.5km
Height gain: 1540ft/470m
Time: 2 hours

From the village car park turn right and follow the narrow lane up the valley. Turn right at the waterfalls bridleway sign, using the direction indication of the signpost as a guide across the field to the next gate. From here the path angles left across another field. A waymark post keeps you on course to the next gate.

At the top of the pasture and beyond another gate there's another signpost. Follow its direction, climbing to the right to a gate giving access to a large pasture low down in Cwm Nantewyn. The route stays low at first, keeping some trees and patches of bracken to the right before climbing left towards the foot of the hillslopes on the west side of the cwm – a very shallow hollow highlights the way, though there's no path yet.

Soon you'll see a raised section of the route lined by bracken, and when there's a fork in the new track take the higher, left one. This leads to another wooden gate (GR 019277), beyond which the path descends a short way.

The route from here is an ancient one, sometimes choked with rushes. Narrow trods, more often than not very faint, continue NNW with a small grass-and-bracken ravine, and a fence to the right. Eventually the path crosses the ravine and its tiny stream before going through a gate in the fence on the other side (GR 017280).

Further narrow trods lead northwards over grassland towards the ridge to join another bridleway at a gate (GR 016285) in a fence not shown on current OS maps. A clear path now continues to the gate on the Hafod Hir ridge fence. Turn left and follow the fence across short-cropped heather, rough grass and moss. It's hard walking, but not by Hirnant standards.

Eventually the fence joins a cross-fence high on the slopes of Y Groes Fagl. Once over this, head just south of west to the post on its tussocky grass summit.

Descent

By heading due east you'll come across a fence intersection at GR 993292. Once over the cross-fence head ESE alongside the ridge fence ahead, which leads for just short of 2 miles/3.2km to the gate by another fence intersection at GR 016286. Turn right along a clear path to a gate in another cross-fence (not shown on current maps).

The path on the ground through this gate is the eastern one of two bridleways – you will want the western, which is unclear at this stage. Head south with a fence on your left. Go through a gate in this fence before crossing a rushy ravine. A sunken rushy track descends southwards, now with the ravine to the left.

You'll see a good track on the pastured hill ahead. The path climbs up to it and follows it

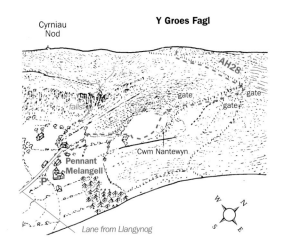

Y Groes Fagl

Cyrniau Nod

falls

gate
gate
gate

Cwm Nantewyn

Pennant Melangell

P

Lane from Llangynog

through a gate. You've now left the moor behind and look down sloping green pastures. The track gives up a short way beyond a second gate, but be content to just head southwards towards a line of trees at the bottom of the field. Now turn right at the field-edge.

Go over a stile with a bridleway signpost. The bridleway is now waymarked and heads south-east, then south, across fields to the road just west of the church and car park.

Other route options

You could begin the route at Llangynog and use lanes and tracks up Cwm Rhiwarth to meet Route AH20 from Milltir Gerrig at the valley head.

RIDGE ROUTES

Foel Cwm Sian-llwyd

Distance: 1¼ miles/2.8km
Height gain: 215ft/65m
Time: 1 hour

This is an ill-defined, heather-tangled and peat-bogged ridge with little to recommend it. There are no paths to help you across sometimes very rough terrain. The ridge is broad and there's no ridge fence, so don't bother even attempting this one in mist.

Route description here is superfluous – keep north along the high ground. There are two low fences to cross and a marshy col known quite aptly as Bwlch y Dwr, the pass of the water. On meeting the old highway (a sunken track in the heather), a narrow path does develop, climbing to Foel Cwm Sian-llwyd's trig point.

Cyrniau Nod

Distance: ¾ mile/1.2km
Height gain: 100ft/30m
Time: ½ hour

Head south on a little path, which joins a forestry track at the apex of a sharp bend. Follow the bulldozed track southwards to another sharp right-hand bend. Just beyond this (at GR 988286) turn left on a narrow path that comes to a fence and follows it to the right to an intersection of fences. Turn left (south) and follow the narrow path alongside the fence (now on the right) to the pole and cairn on Cyrniau Nod's summit.

Pen Cerrig

Distance: 3¼ miles/5.2km
Height gain: 165ft/50m
Time: 1½–2 hours

Descend eastwards across heather and peat to a fence intersection at GR 993292. Go over the low cross-fence before following the ridge fence ahead, keeping it to your left. The terrain is tussocky grass and heather. The broad featureless ridge is quite hard going but by Hirnant standards not that hard.

After a gate where you cross a bridleway (linking Cwm Rhiwarth to Cwm Pennant), keep following the fence ahead up a slight rise in the ridge. The ridge with its fence then gradually veers to the south, and narrows; here you may be tempted to detour to the crag fringe on the north-east (Cwm Rhiwarth) side.

After another dip the fence leads to the summit of Craig Boeth (marked as Waun Bwlchmynydd on the map) before coming to the lower but more interestingly craggy top of Pen Cerrig.

Opposite: Cwm Pennant, at the start of Route AH28.

Pen Cerrig, the hill of stones, is the most prominent though not the highest of a long ridge separating the serenely beautiful valleys of Cwm Rhiwarth and Cwm Pennant. You may wonder why I have chosen this and not the higher Hafod Hir as the main summit of the ridge, but you won't when you arrive.

Hafod Hir is featureless and tussocky, no more than an afterthought on Y Groes Fagl's south-east ridge, while Pen Cerrig is blessed with fine cliffs on the Cwm Rhiwarth side and superb rocky tors overlooking Cwm Pennant. These offer splendid perches to view the surrounding mountainscapes, which include the high Berwyn, the Hirnant ridges and the rounded hills of Shropshire and Radnor.

Route AH29
Llangynog and Nant yr Henglawdd
A fine route beneath the crags
Start: Llangynog village car park
   (GR: SJ 053262)
Distance: 3¼ miles/5.2km
Height gain: 1280ft/390m
Time: 1¾ hours

From the village car park turn left along the road past the New Inn before turning right on the lane signed Pennant Melangell. Almost immediately afterwards turn right again along a narrow lane winding into Cwm Rhiwarth beneath the cliff-fringed ridge of Y Gribin. After passing an outlying small housing estate the lane delves into a delightful rural valley, with the Afon Eirth down on your right beyond hedgerow and woodland copses.

Opposite: The summit of Pen Cerrig looking to Cyrniau Nod.
Below: Pen Cerrig's ridge in winter.

If you're in a hurry to get to the hills you can follow a complex footpath beginning at the gate on the near side of Buarth-glas farm (not signed at the roadside). To do this go through the gate and go straight ahead on a grass track to a waymarked stile by a shed. The waymarked streamside path climbs to the larch woods at the foot of the slopes, where it will meet the main route.

The main route uses the signed bridleway, which begins further along the lane by a gate at GR 035282. It climbs diagonally left across fields, passing through gates at field boundaries, to reach the gate at the edge of the access area. Once through this the bridleway follows a fence on the left, with the cottages of Buarth-glas below.

As it nears the stream, Nant Buarth Glas, the path gingerly takes to the lower bracken slopes and can get a little lost in midsummer vegetation. Remember that you're aiming for the larch trees beneath the rocks of Craig Pen-y-buarth. The best way to avoid the thickest of the bracken is to stay close to the stream to reach the bridleway gate by the stream crossing at GR 035273 (it's a little higher up the slope than the line would show on the current map).

From here enter the small plantation of larch trees. They're well spaced trees, too, so there's no problem in descending through them to the wide grassy track running along the bottom edge of the woods. This leads back on to the open fell.

From here a splendid track angles south up the slopes, with the craggy fringe of Craig Pen-y-buarth above you. The track reaches the ridge and doubles back up to the right to follow the ridge fence; but you leave it to go through the bridleway gate in this fence and climb along the fence's far side. Go over another gate at a fence intersection near the top of the fell and find yourself a crag to sit on.

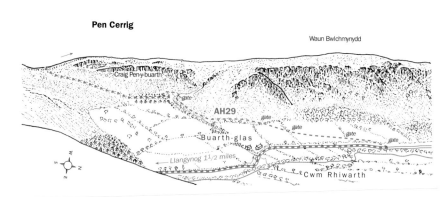

276

Above: Descending from Pen Cerrig by Nant Buarth-glas.

Descent

Descend south-east alongside the ridge fence to the signed wooden bridleway gate. Once through this, join the grassy track raking down the slopes beneath Craig Pen y Buarth into a small larch plantation. The track eventually leads out of the woods at the bottom corner, but the bridleway gate in the fence ahead lies uphill a bit. So the best way is to leave the track for a narrow path that climbs the short way to the top edge of the woods, from where you'll see this gate.

Beyond it the slopes are thickly clad with bracken, which will be shoulder high in summer. To avoid this follow the far banks of Nant Buarth Glas (stream) downhill to a fence corner high above the Buarth-glas cottages. Now you'll see a narrow path on the left, which follows a fence along the bottom edge of the access land.

Eventually the waymarked route enters the fields and works its way diagonally down them to a roadside gate, with gates at all the field edges. Turn right down the lane for Llangynog.

Other route options

There are many options. A route to the ridge leaving the Cwm Rhiwarth road at GR 047264 is signed with a Ty Gofal waymarker, but in reality is the bridleway shown on the map. It climbs diagonally across the field with the spoil of the mine levels directly ahead. Just past the spoil heaps in a wooded area you cross into access land. By turning right and hopping over a low fence you enter the mining area and follow a fence on the right up the hill.

Eventually you join a track (not shown on current maps), which angles up the craggy mountainside. Take the upper left fork at the junction and follow the track as it fords Nant yr Henglawdd before zigzagging up the hillside with crags to the right. The track fizzles out just below the ridge but it's a simple climb to the ridge fence. Turn right along the fence to reach the summit.

There are also options from the car park by Pennant Melangell church in Cwm Pennant. You could take the signed path heading ESE to the forest at Lechwedd-y-garth farm, where a zigzag bridleway climbs to the top edge of the plantation before climbing directly up steep slopes to the bridleway gate on the ridge. Turn left for the summit.

RIDGE ROUTE

Y Groes Fagl

Distance: 3¼ miles/5.2km
Height gain: 720ft/220m
Time: 2 hours

This is a long slog but fairly simple as a ridge fence takes you right to the east shoulder of Y Groes Fagl, where you climb just south of west to reach the pole on the summit. The terrain is generally of tussocky grass with more heather after Hafod Hir.

Opposite: Descent on the alternative route to the quarries at Llangynog.
Above: Llangynog and the Tanat Valley from the slopes of Pen Cerrig.

The bare hill of Sian's grey valley, which is how Foel Cwm Sian-llwyd is translated, is the eastern outlier of the Hirnant group. It lies just west of the Llangynog–Bala road at Milltir Gerrig, and throws out four heathery ridges, two each to the north and the south of the summit.

An older highway linking Llangynog and Bala climbs over the high west shoulder of the mountain. Just a sunken track these days, sometimes not even that, the old highway would have been busy with traders, including drovers and horse-drawn coaches.

Although there are many good ways on to this summit, including the old road, off-path routes are dreadfully rough and thick with heather. What may look like a good ridge-walk to Cyrniau Nod is far from it – it is a horrible slog against the grain of the land.

The summit has a trig point protruding from a sea of heather, looking out across the vast Penllyn Forest to the more familiar giants of Northern Snowdonia. Nearby are the ruins of an old stone-built hut. To the south are two magnificent glacially sculpted valleys, Cwm Rhiwarth and Cwm Pennant. Both have fine waterfalls tumbling from the rock-fringed moors to beautifully pastured valley floors.

Route AH30

Llangynog and Cwm Rhiwarth

An ancient highway past crags and waterfalls to the high moor

Start: Llangynog village car park (GR: SJ 053262)

Distance: 5¼ miles/8.5km

Height gain: 1770ft/540m

Time: 2½–3 hours

From the village car park turn left then right, on the lane signed Pennant Melangell, before turning right shortly afterwards to follow the minor road into Cwm Rhiwarth. This pleasant lane hugs the foot of Hafod Hir's rock-fringed eastern slopes and terminates at GR 032286, where a metalled farm lane leads on to Blaen-rhiwarth farm.

Here a rutted track to the right leads to an old green road, which, until the last century, used to be the main highway between Llangynog and Bala. It climbs on a delectable course parallel to the river and its more modern counterpart on the slaty slopes above and to the right. Soon the waterfalls at the head of the valley come into view. The white plumes rustle in a shady ravine among crag, bracken, rowan and hawthorn.

Above the falls, you'll encounter a track to Milltir Gerrig (which means milestone). The old Bala road we're looking for, marked as a public footpath on the map, has been

Opposite: Foel Cwm Sian-llwyd and Cwm Rhiwarth.

blocked off in two places in the early stages, but as this is access land we can reach it by turning left and fording the stream by a copse of spruce trees.

Now turn right on a faint track climbing parallel to the stream. This meets the old road at GR 013299 just beyond its river crossing. It climbs across increasingly wild terrain to reach a large rustic stile at the old Gwynedd–Powys county boundary. Beyond, we traverse a marshy stretch of moorland characterised by its pale grasses.

A rutted track, still the old Bala road, then continues across deep heather, which is so typical of these wild Hirnant hills. On reaching the ridge, from where the conifers of Penllyn Forest come into view, head north across pathless heather to the summit of Foel Cwm Sian-llwyd.

Above: The summit of Foel Cwm Sian-llwyd.

Foel Cwm Sian-llwyd

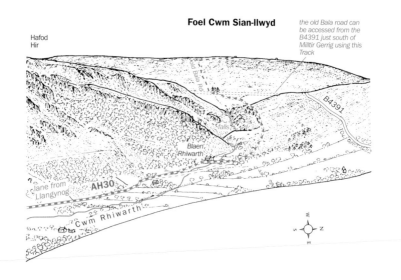

the old Bala road can be accessed from the B4391 just south of Milltir Gerrig using this Track

Hafod Hir

B4391

falls

Blaen Rhiwarth

AH30

lane from Llangynog

Cwm Rhiwarth

Route AH31
Cwm Hirnant and the old Bala road

*A fine route on an historic road which avoids
the forest*

Start: Aber Hirnant picnic site
(GR: SH 957327)

Distance: 3¼ miles/5.2km

Height gain: 1345ft/410m

Time: 1¼ hours

Take the left fork road climbing away out of
Cwm Hirnant to the impressive manor farmhouse of Maes-hir – note the clock tower in
the buildings to the left as you pass through
the courtyard. Through a gate at the far end of
the complex, an old track climbs up to the
pass of Bwlch y Fenni, where you should go
through a gate on the right and follow the
lower of two tracks.

*Above: On the old Bala road heading north
towards Foel Cwm Sian-llwyd.*

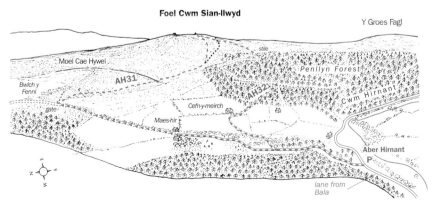

Foel Cwm Sian-llwyd

Y Groes Fagl

stile

Moel Cae Hywel

Penllyn Forest

AH31

Bwlch y
Fenni

AH32

Cwm Hirnant

gate

Cefn-y-meirch

Maes-hir

Aber Hirnant

P

lane from
Bala

This delightful old green road, once the main Bala to Llangynog highway, rakes across the slopes of Moel Cae-Howell before descending slightly to the edge of Penllyn Forest. The track soon becomes sunken and rush-filled, and a convenient if narrow path runs alongside it, never far away from those conifers in the early stages.

By now the heather slopes of Foel Cwm Sian-llwyd are dominant in the view ahead. The odd waymarker post highlights the old road, but watch out for a narrow path on the left, which climbs ESE to the summit.

Route AH32
Cwm Hirnant and Penllyn Forest

Easy walking on forest tracks, followed by pathless heather slopes

Start: Aber Hirnant picnic site
(GR: SH 957327)
Distance: 3 miles/4.7km
Height gain: 1280ft/390m
Time: 1½ hours

Take the left fork road climbing away out of Cwm Hirnant, then leave this for a right fork track past the farm at Cefn-y-meirch and into the spruce woods of Penllyn Forest. Stay with the main track, which climbs steadily ESE keeping north of the Nant Hir then Nant y Sarn streams. Near the top of the plantation the forestry track makes a U-turn, but by leaving it here for a straight-on course though a short fire-break you come to a step stile on to the open fell (GR 989312).

A faint track develops and leads to the crumbling ruins of an old shepherds' hut. The route crosses the sunken path of the old Bala road before making a beeline for the summit. Climb the heather slopes to the ridge before turning left to the summit trig point.

Other route options

There is a direct route from the Llangynog–Bala road (B4391) 2 miles/3.2km north of the Milltir Cerrig pass at GR 006322 – there's a turn-in for cars. It begins on a short grass track which used to serve a remote cottage. Where the track fizzles out use sheep trods, which eventually come to the stream leading you to the heathery, peat-hagged summit plateau – there are helpful sheep tracks and gulleys for most of the way. By angling left (south-west) you should find the summit trig point.

RIDGE ROUTE

Y Groes Fagl

Distance: 1 ¾ miles/ 2.8km
Height gain: 245ft/75m
Time: 1 hour

You could make your way across an ill-defined heather and peat-bogged ridge to Y Groes Fagl, but it wouldn't be worthwhile. There are no paths to help you and Y Groes Fagl has no new views – just the dull, inky-green spread of Hirnant Forest to divert your attention from the heather that tangles around your boots and deposits last year's slightly prickly dead leaves in your socks. The route would also be difficult to navigate in mist.

For those of you who must go, try to find the grassy channels between the heather – they're wetter, but don't try to trip you up so often. There are two low fences to cross and the ridge turns from south-west to south beyond the marshy col known quite aptly as Bwlch y Dwr, pass of the water.

Below: The shelter to the north of Foel Cwm Sian-llwyd's trig point.

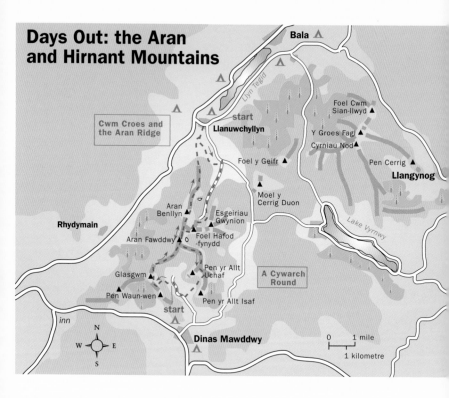

Days Out: the Aran and Hirnant Mountains

Bala

Llyn Tegid

Foel Cwm
Sian-llwyd

start
Llanuwchyllyn

Y Groes Fagl

Cwm Croes and
the Aran Ridge

Cyrniau Nod

Pen Cerrig

Foel y Geifr

Llangynog

Moel y
Cerrig Duon

Aran
Benllyn

Esgeiriau
Gwynion

Lake Vyrnwy

Rhydymain

Aran Fawddwy

Foel Hafod
-fynydd

Glasgwm

Pen yr Allt
Uchaf

A Cywarch
Round

Pen Waun-wen

start

Pen yr Allt Isaf

inn

N
W   E
S

Dinas Mawddwy

0   1 mile

1 kilometre

Days Out: the Aran and Hirnant Mountains

Cwm Croes and the Aran Ridge

*A long but splendid route taking in the best
    parts of the great Aran ridge*

Start: Llanuwchllyn (GR: SH 898298)

Distance: 13 miles/21km

Height gain: 3525ft/1075m

Time: 8–9 hours

---

*Note: If you're based at Bala, the walk could
start and finish with a train ride on the Bala
Lake narrow-gauge railway to and from
Llanuwchllyn, otherwise start at the car
park in Llanuwchllyn.*

The route starts low and will take you down
Cwm Croes (the corrie of the cross) over a
wild pass on the east side of the great Aran
ridge.

From the car park, turn left to the road
corner by the bridge over the Afon Twrch. Go
over the ladder stile on the near side of the
bridge and continue along the farm track
ahead. This winds across fields with the
craggy Aran peaks to the right. Ignore a track
(the Aran ridge route) on the right but stay
with the main track as it passes beneath the
rocks of Garth Fach.

After passing Garth Uchaf, the track
reaches the farming complex at Plas Morgan
– the house, once owned by Peter Price, son
of a high seas buccaneer, has now been
demolished. You should turn left at the near

side of the buildings to descend towards the
Afon Twrch, before which you veer right to
cross a stream and a partially hidden stile
next to a gate.

Beyond a second stile the route heads
south-east over rough pastures and across
footbridges over feeder streams to Cae-poeth
farm. Turn right by the barn at the far end of
the farmyard and climb southwards with
some ruined buildings on the skyline.

After scaling a stile, hidden until the last
moment by a huge rock, turn left (south-east),
following a line of trees across pastureland
high above the river.

Tyn-y-cae farm (GR 892268) is kept to the
left as the path turns left to pass in front of the
main farmhouse and across the access drive
before maintaining direction along the field-
edge on the right. This leads to a track heading right to the Cwm Croes lane.

Cwm Croes is flanked by the grassy hillslopes of Esgeiriau Gwynion to the east,
while to the west the dark crags of Aran Benllyn rise above the green fields of this very
pretty valley, scattered with trees. It is especially beautiful when the hawthorn blooms in
spring.

The right of way leaves the road just south
of Nant-y-barcut farm on a track to the left,
which passes to the right of some ruined outbuildings. The route continues across fields
descending alongside a hedge towards a

copse of conifers, to reach the uninhabited buildings of Cwm-ffynnon.

After traversing some marshy, rush-infested ground beyond Cwm-ffynnon the path, faint to non-existent on the ground at first, strikes for the hills, raking up the eastern flanks of Cwm Ddu, and aiming for the dark conical crag to the left of the cascade at the head of the valley – take a compass bearing (south) if it is misty.

The scenery around Craig Cwm-du becomes more imposing. Beneath the slaty crags and precipitous slopes, the outlines of an old settlement form an interesting foreground to the great Aran cliffs. The old highway comes to Bwlch Sirddyn, a wild marshy pass with the steep grassy flanks of Esgeiriau Gwynion on your left and the equally steep grassy flanks of Foel Hafod-fynydd on your right.

To avoid descending with the track to Dinas Mawddwy you must now leave it to strike for the hills. The direct way by the fence ahead to Foel Hafod-fynydd is too steep for comfort and it is better to contour south-east above the marshes of Gors Lwyd before climbing west to the ridge. Once on the crest a fence will guide you along the ridge, past the white rocks of the summit cairn.

Foel Hafod-fynydd is a wonderful viewpoint for the Aran's eastern crags and cliffs, which stretch along the horizon. Below them is Creiglyn Dyfi, the source of one of Wales's great rivers, the Dyfi. The east face is interrupted just to the north of the lake by a gracefully arced grassy spur, Erw y Ddafad-ddu. This will be the route to the ridge.

The route descends, by the fence at first then on open hill, down to the little col at the head of Cwm Llwydd. Although steep, the

Opposite: Llyn Lliwbran from above.
Above: The magnificent grass spur of Erw y Ddafad-ddu.
Overleaf: Llyn Tegid and Bala from Aran Benllyn's north ridge.

route up Erw y Ddafad-ddu is stimulating, with Aran Fawddwy's great crags now displaying fine sculptured detail and the sheltered waters of the lake rippling with the reflected sky.

Once you reach the ridge fence there's just a short there-and-back detour on steep bouldery slopes to the south to take in Aran Fawddwy's views. A narrow stone-built trig point caps the rocks of the range's highest summit. Creiglyn Dyfi now lies almost hidden beneath the cliffs, but looking south Cadair Idris becomes prominent in views, as do the bell-shaped outlines of the Rhinog peaks.

Retrace your steps north along the rocky ridge, which continues to Aran Benllyn, passing the odd pool en route. Benllyn adds a new perspective to Fawddwy's views, for Llyn Tegid (Bala Lake) can be seen end on, stretch-

ing among the green fields of the Dee Valley, framed by the peaks of Arenig Fawr, Foel Goch and the Berwyn. Unfortunately, Benllyn's own little lake, Llyn Lliwbran, is out of sight tucked tightly beneath the cliffs of Craig y Llyn, but you do get glimpses of it as the route descends north past Llyn Pen Aran and a smaller pool just to the north.

The path continues northwards, keeping to the west of the ridge for much of the time but occasionally rejoining the crest. Finally you pass to the left of little Garth Fach, a crag-topped, pastured hill. Beyond this the route turns right across fields before coming to the farm lane used on the outward route. This leads back to the bridge at Llanuwchllyn where you might see the plumes of smoke from one of the Bala Lake Railway's little steam trains.

A Cywarch Round

*A thoroughly stimulating walk with great
   crags, fine ridges and beautifully verdant
   valleys*

Start: Cwm Cywarch car park
   (GR: SH 853187)

Distance: 10½ miles/17km

Height gain: 3510ft/1070m

Time: 6–7 hours

Cwm Cywarch is one of Snowdonia's greatest secrets, a verdant valley, which at first has great pastoral beauty, with gentle hills, a frisky tree-enshrouded stream and attractive farm cottages. An extremely narrow and winding lane takes you through all this before terminating at Blaencywarch, the head of the valley.

Here the beauty is savage. Spectacular and dramatic climbers' cliffs, crags, gulleys and gorges soar from the lush fields and woods to the now confined skies. Here is great mountain architecture – you just have to get your boots on and get among it.

The route begins on an old quarry track taking you up among the cliffs before traversing the Aran's southern ridges. Turn right out of the car park and follow the lane to the flat common of Fawnog Fawr before angling off to the right along a stony vehicle track. This fords a stream (the ford can be difficult after heavy rain) and continues past the cottage of Gesail and a ruin beyond it.

Note that the right of way marked on the map hasn't existed on the ground for a long time and has been replaced in practice with

Opposite: The old quarry track out of Cwm Cywarch.
Above: The crags of Cwm Cywarch.

the track you're on. (It would have crossed the horrible field of rushes you see half-left and continued on a narrow spur between two streams that is now choked with head-high bracken.)

The now grassy track winds up the hillside. There is great contrast between the verdant slopes of Pen Waun-wen along with the soft greenery of surrounding trees and the buttresses of Craig Cywarch; and it's with regret that you leave it behind when the track ends as it nears the col.

On reaching the col, climb right and go over the step stile near a fence intersection. Do not cross the adjacent ladder stile but follow the narrow path near the cliff edge. (In bad ice, snow or mist follow the fence until GR 837188, where it bends left, then head north to the summit.) The path climbs north, then the gradients ease and temporarily you find yourself on a high moorland walk. Only the rocky outlines of Aran Fawddwy in the mid-distance give away the true story.

The path leads to a large tarn, Llyn y Fign. Go over the stile in the fence to the right of the lake and continue north for Glasgwm's huge summit cairn, where wide views north-westwards across the hedgerows and pastures of the Wnion valley lead the eye to the Rhinogydd and the Mawddach Estuary, which can be seen over the shoulder of Cadair Idris and its foothills.

The high route continues north-west by a fence down slopes of easy grass and crag to reach a marshy col, where the old traders' route between Rhydymain and Cwm Cywarch crosses the hill. Now Aran Fawddwy lies ahead, its pale crag-interspersed grass slopes rising steadily but unspectacularly (from here) to the skies. Still by the fence, a path climbs on to them.

The path from Drysgol and Drws Bach joins in from the right, and the mountainscapes become filled with drama again, with glimpses down rocky precipices to the tarn of Creiglyn Dyfi. Soon you're standing by the stone-built summit trig point enjoying the view towards Bala's lake, which stretches like a pale blue ribbon across equally pallid farm pastures. It's time to start the journey back.

Retrace your steps only as far as the previously mentioned path junction. This time go over the stile and take the left fork down towards Drws Bach. The cliffs of Aran Fawddwy's east face and the lake can be seen to good vantage as you come to the memorial cairn on Drws Bach. Both sides of the mountain are precipitous as you descend a narrow ridge then go up the short slope to Drysgol.

Again the drama recedes and the path bends to the right around the head of Hengwm, a deep but wet green hollow. Don't follow the clear path down into Hengwm but climb south on wettish ground on to Waun Goch, where you should head south-west along a ridge to a fence intersection at GR 872197.

Here turn left to follow the fence around the head of Cwm Terwyn and towards a forest corner. Where the fence veers a little left leave it and head south-east with a rounded knoll by a sharp forest corner featuring directly ahead (585m spot height).

Watch out for a faint rushy groove on the right beneath the knoll. This is the start of the old track down Cwm Terwyn – the line can quite clearly be seen ahead as it's highlighted by rushes.

Near the bottom of the cwm waymarking arrows direct you off the track and down to a wooden bridge over Nant Terwyn, then left above the far banks of the stream. Over two ladder stiles the route comes to some farm outbuildings shaded by trees.

Turn left on a track crossing a stone bridge taking you back over the stream, past the farmhouse and out to the Cywarch road, where you turn right back up Cwm Cywarch. By now the crags at the head of the valley will be in shade and slightly menacing, but all this is softened by the pretty country lane winding among meadows and trees back to the car park.

Above: Aran Fawddwy from Drysgol.
Overleaf: View from the quarry track by Craig Cywarch looking down the verdant valley of Hengwm

MAPS

Ordnance Survey Explorer (1:25,000)
    OL 18 Snowdonia: Harlech,
    Porthmadog/Bala
    OL 23 Cadair Idris & Llyn Tegid
    Sheet 255 Llangollen & Berwyn
Ordnance Survey Landranger (1:50,000)
    Sheet 124 Porthmadog & Dolgellau
    Sheet 125 Bala & Lake Vyrnwy
    Sheet 135 Aberystwyth & Machynlleth

TRANSPORT

Buses

The D79 (Tanat Valley Coaches) service from Oswestry and Chirk to Llangynog helps with routes on to the southern Hirnant hills, while the regular X94, from Wrexham to Barmouth via Bala, Rhydymain and Dolgellau, is useful for some Hirnant routes and the north-western approaches to the Aran mountains.

Routes 30, 32 and 33 from Dolgellau serve Corris, Minffordd, Abergynolwyn, Tywyn, Dinas Mawddwy and Machynlleth. They can get you to some of the start points for southern approaches to Cadair Idris and northern approaches to the Tarren Hills and the Dyfi Hills around both Dinas Mawddwy and Corris.

Service no. 28 runs from Dolgellau to Aberystwyth via Tywyn, Aberdyfi, Cwrt, Pennal and Machynlleth and is useful for the southern Tarren peaks.

Bus timetable:
    www.gwynedd.gov.uk/bwsgwynedd

Trains

There's a mainline railway linking
    Porthmadog and Machynlleth (for onward
    trains to Aberystwyth and Shrewsbury) by
    way of Fairbourne, Tywyn and Aberdyfi.
    The Morfa Mawddach station on this
    line is well placed for the western ridges
    of Cadair Idris. At Tywyn the Tal-y-llyn
    narrow-gauge railway runs to
    Abergynolwyn (Nant Gwernol)
    via Bryncrug and Dolgoch – excellent
    for the Tarren hills.
Rail travel timetable (Railtrack):
    www.nationalrail.co.uk
For more information: www.traveline-
    cymru.org.uk

ACCOMMODATION AND SUPPLIES

Tourist Information Centres (year round)
Bala
    Tel. 01678 521021
    Email: bala.tic@gwynedd.gov.uk
Dolgellau
    Tel. 01341 422888
    Email: tic.dolgellau@eryri-npa.gov.uk
Machynlleth
    Tel. 01654 702401
    Email: mactic@powys.gov.uk

Websites
Welsh Tourist Board: www.visitwales.com
Snowdonia Information:
    www.visitsnowdonia.info
Accommodation: www.4tourism.com

BEST BASES

Bala Bala is very central for much of the region and has a good deal of accommodation ranging from a private hostel, several campsites, through to fine hotels and country houses. It has a small gear shop, and a couple of small supermarkets. The town makes an ideal base for the Hirnant and northern Aran mountains.

Corris This small village in the forest just off the A487 between Dolgellau and Machynlleth has limited accommodation, which includes the independent Corris Hostel based in the old school, a bunkhouse at the Braich Goch Hotel and a hotel (the Dulas Valley).

Dolgellau Beautifully sited beneath Cadair Idris, Dolgellau is a charming country town built from stone and slate. It has plentiful accommodation, including campsites, hotels and B&Bs. It is also well served by public transport. It's a good base for Cadair Idris and the Dyfi hills.

Llangynog Once a thriving lead mining resort and terminus of the Tanat Valley Railway, Llangynog is well placed for exploring the Hirnant peaks. There are two inns and a campsite.

Machynlleth While it's to the south of the area and a couple of miles outside Snowdonia on the banks of the Dyfi river, Machynlleth has good transport links and is well placed for the southern Tarren Hills and not far from the Dyfi Hills. It's a lively if small market town with plenty of shops – some quite unusual ones, too. There are many hotels and B&Bs.

Tywyn Although well sited and reasonably provided with shops, hotels and B&Bs, Tywyn is suffering in the same way as many of Britain's Victorian seaside resorts due to a lack of long-stay visitors. As a result it's a little dog-eared in places. However, it's nice to take in the sea air after a day on the mountains, and there are good transport links for walks on the peaks of both Cadair Idris and the Tarren.

YOUTH HOSTELS

Dolgellau (Penmaenpool)
Kings, Penmaenpool LL40 1TB
Tel. 0845 371 9327
Email: kings@yha.org.uk

YHA National Office
Trevelyan House, Dimple Road, Matlock,
    Derbyshire DE4 3YH
Tel. 0870 770 8868
Website: www.yha.org.uk

THE WELSH LANGUAGE

Some Welsh words

aber	river mouth
afon	river
arddu	black crag
bach/fach	small
bedd	grave
betws	chapel
blaen	head of valley
bont/pont	bridge
bwlch	pass
bws	bus
cae	field
caer	fort
carn/carnedd/garn/garnedd	cairn/cairns
capel	chapel
carreg/garreg	stone
castell	castle
cefn	ridge
cors/gors	bog
clogwyn	cliff
coch/goch	red
coeden/coed	tree/wood
craig/graig	crag
crib	sharp ridge
cwm	coomb
cwn	dog
Cymru/Cymraeg	Wales/Welsh
dinas	hill fort (or town)
diolch	thank you
du/ddu	black
drum/trum	ridge
drws	door
dyffryn	valley
dwr	water
eglwys	church
esgair	ridge
eryri	eagles' abode
fawr/mawr	large
felin/melin	mill
ffordd	road
ffynnon	spring
ffridd	enclosed grazing land
glas/las	blue
gwrydd	green
gwyn	white
gwynt	wind
hafod	high-altitude summer dwelling
hendre	winter dwelling
isaf	lower
llan	church or blessed place
llwybr cyhoeddus	public footpath
llwyd	grey
llyn	lake
maen	stone
maes	field/meadow
melyn	yellow
moch	pig
moel/foel	featureless hill
mynydd	mountain
nant	stream
ogof	cave
pant	clearing, hollow
pen	peak
person	cascade
plas	mansion
pwll	pool
rhaeadr	waterfall
rhyd	ford
saeth(au)	arrow(s)
troed	foot of

twll	hole, fracture, broken
ty	house
uchaf	high, higher
waun	moor
wen	white
wrach	witch
y, yr	the
ynys	island

Pronunciation of consonants

c   always hard, like the English 'k', thus coed = 'koyd'

ch   as in the Scottish 'loch'

dd   a voiced 'th' as in 'booth'

f   like the English 'v' , thus fach = 'vach'

ff   like the English 'f'

ll   a Scots 'ch' followed by an 'l' (blow air out between your tongue and your top teeth when pronouncing)

Pronunciation of vowels

w   can be a consonant or a vowel. When working as a vowel, pronounced like 'oo' as in 'cook' or 'moon'.

y   can be a consonant or a vowel. When working as a vowel, pronounced like 'i' as in pin or 'ee' as in seen. U is exactly the same.

The letters j, k, q, v, x and z are not used in true Welsh words.

INDEX TO PEAKS

(AH) = Aran/Hirnant ranges
(C)= Cadair Idris
(DT)= Dyfi/Tarren ranges